**THE SECRETS BEHIND WHY THE TOP SALESPEOPLE ALWAYS WIN AND HOW <u>YOU</u> CAN BECOME ONE OF THEM.**

# The Millionaire Salesperson

## Dustin W. Ruge

THUNDERBIRD

PUBLISHING

# TABLE OF CONTENTS

• • •

# INTRODUCTION

• • •

*"The difference between something good
and something great is attention to detail."*
— Charles R. Swindoll

At 21 years old, less than a year after he turned pro, Tiger Woods shot a 270 to become the youngest Masters champion in history. Other records Tiger broke that day in 1997 included the largest margin of victory at 12 strokes over second-place finisher Tom Kite—a mere three stroke daily advantage over his nearest competitor over the course of the four-day tournament.

Most people have watched professional golf on TV and continue to marvel at how top players like Tiger Woods, Phil Mickelson, Jordan Spieth, and the like can make what is such a seemingly challenging game to the causal golfer look so easy. The camera crews also lock on to these leaders in each game, making it seem like they are simply light-years ahead of their competition. But in reality, they are not.

The performance difference between the top PGA golfer in the world and the worst is often less than a three-stoke average over the course of a season.[1] That's it! Put another way, over the course of more than 100 games played per year at an average of 70 stokes per game, **the performance difference between the best and the worst is a mere 4 percent.** What this tells us is that the difference between the greatest and worst professional golfers is actually very small. But the rewards are clearly not!

In 2015, 385 golfers earned money on the PGA Tour, ranging from the highest earner—Jordan Spieth—at $12,030,465 to the lowest—Tim Herron—at $5,820.[2] Tim's earnings were less than .0005 percent of Jordan's take, yet the playing performance year after year between the best and the worst players is only around 4 percent. And this doesn't even include the endorsement earnings for the top players, which add up to a great deal more.

So why is this difference important to you? Because this disparity doesn't just exist in golf—the same disparity also exists in sales. And year after year organizations struggle to find an answer to how they can produce more top performers.

So what makes the "top" salespeople truly unique and how can I harness and reproduce it? That has been the million-dollar question that millions of people have asked themselves for centuries now. And for good reason: Only a very small percentage of salespeople ever reach the highest levels of achievement. Recent studies out of Sales Benchmark Index now indicate that this gap in production between the top salespeople and all of the rest is actually growing to the point were only 13 percent of salespeople now account for 87 percent of sales revenues.[3]

As a result, increasing numbers of organizations continue to adopt new sales systems and methodologies to help address this gap. These systems range from sales methodology training to the CRM systems that are commonly used to support and gauge performance. With all of these "system improvements," one might assume that the inequality of sales produced would begin to reverse itself—but it has not. Quite the opposite.

There are many very good sales methodologies and systems in use today—and we will discuss many of them in more detail in this book—but that is NOT what this book is about. Rather, the one fundamental flaw in all of these systems is that they are all deployed and managed at the company and organizational levels. In short, we treat our salespeople monolithically and then manage and measure their results in a similar manner. To use an analogy, we are trying to run teams of golfers who can all wear the same clothes and who we can train to "play golf" but who will all eventually produce different results.

This book is about the 4 percent difference that each and every top-performing salesperson brings to the table, and what makes them so unique and successful while the rest continue to fail. We explore the PERSONAL habits, PERSONAL best practices, and the PERSONAL systems developed at the "individual level" of these top performers and why this is where the true level of differentiation and success resides.

I have been working with all types of salespeople for over two decades now, while always looking for the silver bullet in sales. Only recently have I come to the conclusion that most organizations are all looking for the same answer but more often than not in the wrong places. They know who their best salespeople are but they can never seem to clone and reproduce their results in others. The more business systems and processes they deploy at the company level to help address this problem, the worse the resulting separation is becoming.

Now it's time to turn the tide of sales success by looking beyond just business systems to the area where the greatest differentiation of sales success truly resides. In the following chapters, you will learn how the greatest salespeople create the highest levels of differentiation within themselves. When you are done, you will see that the answer we all strive for is truly not beyond us but rather lies within.

# CHAPTER 1

# UNDERSTANDING THE SALES PARADOX

• • •

*"To me, job titles don't matter. Everyone is in sales.*
*It's the only way we stay in business."*
— Harvey Mackay

When I speak to groups of young college graduates I ask them a simple question: "How many people here have dreamed of becoming a millionaire?" Most of the hands go up. I then ask, "Now, how many people here have dreamed of becoming a salesperson?" Most hands go down. And here is my response: "Why?" Most people don't have an answer. In fact, many will laugh and look around for others to answer.

Welcome to the sales paradox.

Whether you are conscious of it or not, every day we are buying and selling—all of us are and all of the time! Whether you are buying and/or selling thoughts, ideas, products, services, yourself, others, etc., you are in a constant persuasion process, which is selling. Want to run a Fortune 500 company one day? Next to finance, the second most common path to getting there starts in sales.[1] Want to own your own business one day? Great! As a result you will likely need to be your top salesperson to help make it initially successful.

But the title "salesman" has negative connotations for most people today because of what we were raised to believe about salespeople through movies and TV. Let's face it: All of us have been "burned" by a salesperson at least once in our lives. This is why companies have become creative in changing the titles of their salespeople to less threatening alternatives such as Account Managers, Customer Success Managers, Customer Specialists, and the like . . . anything but "salesperson." And this tends to work! If you don't believe me, try printing two sets of business cards, one using the title "salesperson" and other titled "Customer Specialist," and see how receptive people initially are to each title used by your salespeople.

Let's face it: Nobody "wants" to become a salesperson. I certainly didn't and I'm sure you didn't, either. Most young children instead dream of becoming actors ($35/hour), astronauts ($64K–$141K/year), dancers ($41K/year), teachers ($30–$58K/year), firefighters ($48K/year), cops ($58K/year), musicians ($32/hour), athletes ($78K/year), veterinarians ($93K/year), etc.[2] The reality is that 70 percent of us **will NEVER end up working in the careers of our childhood dreams.** For the remaining 30 percent who do follow their childhood dreams, many will have to take on debt and student loans just to get to these "non-millionaire" income levels—resulting in even lower "net" income for many.[3]

That is unless you are a great salesperson.

So here is the inconvenient truth: Good sales and marketing professionals are in short supply and high demand in nearly every industry and in any economy. As a result, they are commonly able to command better jobs, earn better pay, receive faster promotions, and have more career options. So if you want to become a millionaire, sales is most likely one of your best paths forward to get there.

But just because you may find a path into sales doesn't necessarily mean you will be successful there. In nearly every industry and business I have been part of, only around 20 percent of the salespeople will account for 80 percent of the sales . . . and income. Welcome to Pareto's Law. It was these top 20 percent among us that inspired me to write my second book, *The Top 20%*, about what made these business professionals so special and successful.

So what are your chances of becoming part of the top 20 percent of salespeople, and what if you are already in sales but haven't yet reached this level of success? Can you still reach this level of success if it has previously eluded you? The answer is "yes," and in this book you will learn about another salesperson who was able to reach this pinnacle of sales success and turn their life around based on the lessons you will learn in this book.

So let's get started by meeting a struggling salesperson named Linda.

# CHAPTER 2

# WHAT IS YOUR PRIMARY PURPOSE

· · ·

*"The two most important days in your life*
*are the day you are born and the day you find out why."*
*— Mark Twain*

I met Linda a number of years ago at a technology company where we both worked. Linda had been in sales for over a decade, which means that most people today would consider her a "seasoned" salesperson. Linda was a mother of two young children and part of what most of us are all too familiar with today—a dual-income "working" family. Her husband had followed his childhood dream of becoming a teacher, and based on their location and desired lifestyle, Linda had no choice but to earn extra income to help support her family . . . which led her into sales.

When Linda first walked into my office, I remembered back to a book I'd read years before about body language and how to better read people based on how they first present themselves. Linda was a textbook example of what to look out for.

"Hi, Dustin; my name is Linda," she said as she first approached my desk to shake my hand. There was little eye contact when our hands first met and her handshake was as firm and convincing as a wet sponge.

"Nice to meet you, Linda. Please have a seat," I responded.

Linda quickly sat down, started to fidget, and seemed nervous. I could tell this meeting was not comfortable for her, so I asked, "Is everything okay?"

"Yes, everything is great," she responded. "I'm excited to have you as my new boss."

Her new boss. Now, that is a title that never sat well with me. In all my years in business, I never once considered myself to be anybody's boss. I have worn many hats ranging from salesperson to business owner, all of which required different responsibilities. But at no time did I ever feel comfortable with the negative connotations that I personally connected with this title. So far, this meeting was not starting off well.

"Linda, I see you have been with the company for about five years, and since we will now be working together, I wanted to have us get to know each other a little better," I said.

"Great," Linda responded, and placed a copy of her résumé on the desk in front of me.

I briefly looked down at it and, leaving it there, said, "Let's talk a little more about you before we get into your résumé. Does that work for you?"

"Okay," said Linda with a rather puzzled look on her face.

What Linda didn't know was that I had already done my "résumé homework" on her and the rest of the salesforce at the company before our meeting. As with nearly all underperforming salespeople, Linda was ready to try to explain her underperformance at the company with me. Her track record at the company was pretty clear:

- Linda had failed to achieve her sales quota three out of her last five years.

- Linda had never achieved a President's Club level of sales performance at the company.

- Linda was not part of the company's top 20 percent of sales producers.

Linda's was one of the last meetings I had with the sales and sales management teams. Being one of the last meetings certainly wouldn't help anybody's confidence—especially when the usual "coffee talk" took place after each of the preceding meetings. I'm sure this made Linda even more nervous and concerned, but what happened next surprised her.

"Linda, can you tell me about your children?" I asked. "I see you have a lot of pictures at your desk area and those have to be some of the cutest kids I have ever seen." Linda could not believe her ears and her mood suddenly changed from fear and apprehension to excitement and joy.

There are only 168 hours in a week and most good salespeople will spend around 50 of those hours (or 30 percent of their life) working. Accounting for another 56 hours for sleep (33 percent of their time), this means that most people are only left with 62 waking hours (37 percent of their remaining time) for everything else, including life and family. In short, **most people spend more time awake at work than they do with their own families.** It was clear that Linda currently had only one primary purpose in her life (her children) and she was not afraid to show it to others. Her problem was that her primary purpose was at home with her children, which is where she was not spending the majority of her time each workday.

Additionally, her accomplishments at work were simply not good and no amount of money could seem to bring her happiness at work. Every year she watched as her coworkers walked up on stage and received awards and promotions while she was stuck in neutral. Something had to change and she knew it. This was apparent in both her body language and her first interactions with me.

Linda is only human, and like all humans she has an inherent need to live a purpose-driven life. It is simply not human nature to spend the majority of our waking hours feeling like nothing is being accomplished in our lives—especially when so many of us live to regret it.

One of the best lessons I received about purpose in life came from a palliative care nurse who spent years working with patients whose lives were nearing their end. During her time caring for these patients, she would ask them if they had any regrets or if there was anything they would have done differently. Here were the most common responses she received:[1]

- I wish I'd had the courage to live a life true to myself, not the life others expected of me.
- I wish I hadn't worked so hard.

- I wish I'd had the courage to express my feelings.
- I wish I had stayed in touch with my friends.
- I wish that I had let myself be happier.

After reading this list of regrets, it's hard for anybody to not look at their own lives and personal situation and ask themselves if they too are on the path to suffering the same fate. In many ways, Linda had been heading down this path whether she was conscious of it or not. Remember: Nobody ever wrote a headstone that read "Made a Lot of Money" followed by "Rest in Peace." These are the tombstone questions each and every one of us must ask ourselves before our time runs out as well and we are left with the same regrets.

The purpose of only "making money" in our work does not create the motivation and passion for our work. This lack of satisfaction and accomplishment was clearly tormenting Linda. But this is nothing new. Studies have shown that upwards of **80 percent of people indicate that they are NOT HAPPY in their current jobs.**[2] This is why hiring for character and trying to make sure that those happy 20 percent of people are working for you or with you is so important.

In the end, the primary motivation for most working people is not money. The military learned the lesson long ago that soldiers of faith fight harder than soldiers of fortune. Why else would people who work for paltry incomes put their lives on the line each day? When Napoleon Bonaparte transformed a battered mercenary French army into one of the most effective and revered fighting forces in Europe he didn't motivate them with money alone. Instead, he used internal motivation recognized through badges, purpose, honor, and country to compel his armies to want to fight harder and win.

"My son's name is Jack and my daughter is Ashley," Linda said with a big smile and a strong sense of pride. "They are my world and I would do anything for them. I drop Jack and Ashley off at school every morning before work and my husband picks them up after school. Do you have any children?"

"Yes, I have two children," I replied. "They mean the world to me as well. That's why I love being in sales."

Linda seemed a little puzzled by my response. Clearly she did not initially understand the association I had made between my children and sales, which is exactly where I wanted to take her in this conversation.

"Linda, when I hire great salespeople I hire for character and train for skills," I said. "The reason for that is because I cannot train character; people either have it or they don't. Based on everything I've heard about you from others, you have great character, which, to me, is the foundation for success.

"All of the best salespeople I've ever worked with had great character, but that alone was only the foundation for their success. All of them also had a primary purpose as well. Many of them also had children like yours who they loved. I even had one salesperson named Ryan who only worked four days a week so he could spend three-day weekends with his kids. He didn't start out that way. In fact, the first year I inherited him he was well below quota, worked obscene hours five days a week, and considered quitting. The next year he decided that four days was right for his work/life balance and ended up as one of the top salespeople in his company that year. Is that something you would like to accomplish one day?"

"Wow, that would be a dream for me," replied Linda. I clearly had her full attention at this point.

"That's the difference, Linda," I replied. "It will always be a dream for you until you define it as a goal and take actions and instill personal accountability in order to achieve it. Ryan decided that his primary purpose was to better support his children and realized that in order to do that, he too needed to be much more successful to support that need. Since Ryan now has success and meaning at both work and at home, he's happier than ever before in both environments. This is what I can help you accomplish in your own personal AND professional life as well, but that purpose and goal must be your own. Once you can commit 100 percent of yourself to that purpose, I can then help you achieve it.

"What is more time with your family worth to you?" I asked. "What would a higher income be worth to you and your children's future? What would winning sales awards be worth to your self-esteem around the office? What would being a consistent President's Club–award winner be worth to your career and future even if one day you decided to work elsewhere?"

At this point, I clearly had Linda's full attention and, more important, I had helped her to start understanding her purpose and exactly how a successful career in sales could help support it.

Sadly, Linda is like most people who go through life failing to understand what their primary purpose is and how to help support it. We live in a society that is largely made up of people whose brains are programmed toward a herding mentality—which helps to instinctively ensure our survival as a species but rarely allows people to think beyond the cultural dogma we are commonly part of.

**This ability to "think critically" is ironically the number one trait companies look for when hiring today, yet seems to be in very short supply.** For many people, this ability to critically think is not encouraged or even developed at our institutions of higher learning and often shows in the ways we lead of lives moving forward.[3]

The old saying that there is "strength in numbers" is true. However, the true benefactor of the herding strength is the leader of the herd. So unless Linda decided that she wanted to define her own purpose and work toward her own goals, dogma would force her to work for others to help them obtain their goals on their terms instead. This is one of the primary reasons the majority of people like Linda get "stuck" in life, and at the end of their lives have more regrets than accomplishments to reflect upon.

Everybody has a primary purpose whether they recognize it or not. Those who recognize it and work toward it are the leaders of the herd and are commonly the people we most admire in all walks of life—including business. Your primary purpose can and likely will evolve as your life matures, but it all starts with awareness. Linda's primary purpose was her children, but it can be many things to many people, ranging from family, income, lifestyle, possessions, etc. Once you are aware of your purpose, you will have the clarity to better lead your life in support of it. Linda knew what was most important to her but, like most people, she was unaware of how best to support it—especially in her career.

"I want to have all those things you mentioned but I just can't seem to get there," replied Linda. "I follow the same sales system the company provides all of our salespeople but I sometimes wonder if sales is just not for me. I sometimes feel like every day is Groundhog Day and there's no end in sight. I even spent a few weeks working with our top salespeople to see if I could learn from them and try to reproduce their success at our company."

"Did it work?" I replied.

"No," said Linda. "That's what's so frustrating. They're following the same sales process and system as I am and I still cannot figure out why their sales numbers are so much higher than mine. A few of these sales reps even work fewer hours than I do yet they're killing it."

"And how does that make you feel?" I asked.

"Hopeless," said Linda.

This is how most salespeople who are not in the top 20 percent feel—whether they care to admit it or not. To Linda's credit, she was honest, had great character, and, most important, she wanted to succeed. Psychologists commonly tell us that the first step in fixing a problem is to admit that a problem exists. Many people who are not successful in sales fail at this first step. Instead of taking ownership of a problem, they blame others and/or circumstances that are out of their control instead of their failures to succeed.

"Linda, I know how you feel," I said. "We have all been there before. One of the first things I tell salespeople is to **worry only about things YOU can control. Any worries beyond that will only lead to disappointment.** When you were working with the top sales reps, you expressed frustration that despite following the same sales system as you, they were putting up better sales results. Was your primary focus then on WHAT they were doing?"

"Yes," replied Linda. "They were doing the same things that I was."

"If you were focused on WHAT they were doing, how much time did you spend on better understanding HOW they were doing it and WHY?"

I asked. "Most people will watch professional golfers, baseball players, and the like and never know that a mere 4 percent improvement in HOW they play can mean the difference between getting cut and becoming a multimillionaire. Sports professionals all know how to swing a club or a bat, yet most people cannot see that 4 percent difference. But it's there and the results clearly show it. When you observed WHAT the top sales reps were doing, you were missing the most important 4 percent of HOW and WHY they were doing it better than you. Because of that, you felt hopeless not because you were not willing to do it, but because you didn't know exactly where to focus on what to do better."

"So how do I find that focus?" replied Linda. "I want to be the best if somebody will show me how to do it."

"Much like a great golfer, you need a swing coach to help you better refine HOW you are working and WHAT you are really working for," I said. "This is where I can help, but I can only help you if you are 100 percent committed to becoming the best salesperson in this company. By becoming the best salesperson, you will then earn the ability to spend more time with your children, just like Ryan did. If you can make that commitment to me and yourself, then I will help you get to that goal. Is that a deal?" I now stood up straight, extended my hand out to Linda, and waited for her response . . .

Linda stood up, reached out with a smile, and shook my hand. Unlike Linda's previous handshake, mine was strong and powerful and I looked Linda in the eye without a flinch. Clearly my body language alone was enough to convince Linda that I was very serious about this. Linda seemed to be both relieved and excited at the same time. She could tell this was a potential tipping point in her career and didn't know exactly how to initially react.

"Wow, thank you so much!" said Linda. "I have never had anybody help me like this and I really look forward to doing much better at work."

"Linda, this is much bigger than your work, for what we are talking about is changing your whole life along with your work," I replied. "So buckle up, and let's get started . . . "

## — CHAPTER 3 —

# BUILDING "PERSONAL" SALES SYSTEMS THROUGH HABITS

• • •

*"We are what we repeatedly do.*
*Excellence, then, is not an act but a habit."*
*— Aristotle*

"But I'm already following the sales system the company told me to follow." This is the answer I hear the most when asking salespeople why they are underperforming. It was nearly the same answer I received from Linda during our first strategy meeting.

"Linda, can I ask you a question?" I responded.

"Of course," replied Linda.

"Who is the top salesperson in the company?" I asked.

"That's easy. It's been Robert for the past three years," she replied.

"So if I were to ask Robert if he was following the same company-provided sales system that you are using, do you think he would give me the same answer?" I asked.

"Yes, I know he would," replied Linda. "I've worked with him a number of times over the past few years and I know for a fact that he uses the same system. I've seen it."

"So if you're both following the same company-provided sales system, why do you think Robert has been significantly outperforming you and the rest of the sales team for the past three years?" I asked.

Linda just sat quietly in her seat, trying to come up with an answer while slowly shaking her head from side to side. It is the question that had been haunting her and nearly all struggling salespeople for centuries, and she didn't have the answer.

"The company's sales system is not the problem. Otherwise you would be right on par with Robert," I replied. "You are looking for answers in the wrong place and clearly focusing on the wrong system."

A long time ago I learned an indisputable lesson that all great businesses are built on great systems. In great businesses people run the systems and the systems run the business. The best and most valuable businesses will develop systems that are scalable and repeatable while producing expected and consistent results. This may sound simple, but when 80 percent of small businesses fail every five years, clearly this is a lesson most people continue to learn the hard way.

A perfect example of business systems success comes from one of the most recognizable fast-food companies in the world: McDonald's. When Ray Kroc created the McDonald's franchise model, he created a turn-key system that anybody could operate as long as they strictly followed the business systems and procedures created by McDonald's for their franchisees. By rigidly following these systems, improvements could then be made at the system level, thereby ensuring consistency and scalability across the entire chain of operations.[1]

Businesses like McDonald's cannot grow without systems, and neither can people. Because of this people are inherently provided with the greatest system manager in the world: the human brain. But as amazing as the human brain is, it cannot help a business to succeed and grow without help. Businesses like McDonald's have created literally thousands of systems and procedures to run every aspect of their business. Without the ability to store and retrieve this knowledge in these systems, the average person could not produce the same results. Moreover, without the ability to know each and every step of a system, there is no systematic way to innovate and improve systems without knowing exactly where those improvements can be made.

But selling to people is not the same as running a McDonald's. As much as organizations would like to create sales systems that can scale and consistently reproduce at the levels of a franchise like McDonald's, they simply cannot. **The sales systems we produce are frequently good on the activity level but typically lack in personal effectiveness.** People are people, and people selling to people, no matter how hard we try to standardize it, will always be a highly interpersonal process.

People are truly an amazing race and scientists still to this day do not fully understand how we function. At the heart of our functions is our brain, and without it we are useless. Now, I know what you must be thinking: "How the hell did a sales book become a dissertation on the human brain? What part of business school teaches about the human brain 101?"

If you want to change YOUR life for the better, it all starts with the creation of successful systems—and YOUR systems are all controlled by the human brain. Because we are constantly overloaded with information at any one time, our brains will control, filter, and act on information in repeatable ways. These ways are called habits, and **nearly 40 percent of all of your habitual actions each day happen subconsciously without you thinking twice about them.**[2] Successful people, whether they know it or not, have developed good habits, while unsuccessful people have developed bad habits. The good news is you can change your habits to become more successful. But once again, this first starts with awareness, which is exactly where I begin with people like Linda.

A number of groundbreaking studies have recently emerged that shed light on what habits successful and not-successful people tend to have. I have also worked with many salespeople over the years and have witnessed my own set of successful and unsuccessful habits for salespeople as well—which we will cover in more detail throughout this book. But let's start by understanding where this all begins.

Each of us is increasingly bombarded with all types of information every day—more information than the human brain can possibly process. Recent studies have shown that the average person now has to process around 105,000 words per day, which equates to around twenty-three words per second while we are awake. Put another way, the average human brain today has to process the equivalent of around thirty-four gigabytes of information a day—which is enough information to overload a laptop computer within a week's time.[3]

Because of this, the human brain processes information differently, with fully 80 percent of its processing power taking place at the sub-conscious level—leaving only 20 percent to your conscious mind to manage. Put another way, **fully four-fifths of all of our daily actions happen without us "actively" thinking about it.**

In the military, this ability to act instinctively and subconsciously is commonly referred to as "muscle memory"—based on the concept of motor memory whereby repetition helps to program the brain to repeat actions and activities at the subconscious level. Because of this, it is not uncommon to hear soldiers recall war stories saying things like, "You don't have time to think. You think and you're dead," or "My training took over." It wasn't the training that took over but rather the human brain, due to its innate survival skills, that made a subconscious decision based on trained information it had received over and over again.

In order to better understand how we use our brains, it is important to understand a little more about them. Over the past seven million years, the human brain has tripled in size, where today our brains are double the size of other mammals of equal body size. And while our brains have grown in size, they've also become more complex—different portions of the brain have now become specialized to handle different functions. Ever heard the term "thinking with your left brain and feeling with your right"? This is actually very true.

The human brain evolved in three general phases. Phase one started with the reptilian brain, which is located at the center of your brain nearest to the spine, and controls the body's vital "instinctive" functions such as breathing, heart rate, balance, etc. Phase two involved the development of the limbic system (or limbic brain), which controls your motivations, emotions, learning, and memory. Phase three involved the creation of the largest portion of your brain, the cerebral cortex, where more advanced and "higher-functions" such as information processing like language, thinking, consciousness, etc., take place.

The cerebral cortex generally divides functions between the right side of the brain, which involves more creatively focused aspects, and the left side of the brain, which is more logically and analytically focused.

One of the best illustrations of the different functions of the human brain working together can be seen in the original *Star Trek* TV series and movies that started back in 1966. In *Star Trek*, there was a cast of main characters who in many ways illustrate the various functions of the brain working together. The science officer, Spock, only thought with logic (left brain) and was incapable of feeling. The doctor, Leonard McCoy, was highly emotional (limbic brain) and frequently argued with the "logical" Spock. In the middle was Captain Kirk, who was highly creative in solving problems (right brain) and frequently relied on his two counterparts to help him make more informed decisions. In many respects, these three characters were a perfect illustration of the three main functions of the human brain—in a much more entertaining format than a book on neurology.

Now that we know a little more about how the human brain works, let's discuss habits and why they are so important to your success in sales. **Habits are formed in the brain to make everything you repeatedly do easier and save the brain from working too hard.** Habits are formed in the basal ganglia, which reside in your limbic system (where your emotions are governed). In many ways, like with computers, habits are programmed into the brain to run a set actions.

Whether you know it or not, you have developed many habits already and simply don't realize it each day. Ever sat in the same seat in a room over and over again without knowing exactly why? These habits allow you to subconsciously think, behave, act, and make decisions every minute of your life. These programmed repetitions, such as how you brush your teeth, drive a car, eat, drink, etc., happen over and over again without having to overtax your brain with consciously thinking about all the details.

**Many of our habits come from our parents and are developed before the age of nine.**[4] This is why developing good habits and proper parenting is so important to having a successful career and life. The good news for those of us who were not so fortunate to have a strong upbringing is that you can still change your habits for the better. The first step in changing habits, however, is to recognize which habits can help you in sales and which ones can work against you.

The following are generally considered to be **good habits:**

- Daily exercise
- Daily educational reading
- Proper eating and diet
- Getting at least 7–8 hours of sleep a night
- Efficient use of time
- Always asking for a close during every sale
- Strong verbal and non-verbal communication skills
- Thinking positive thoughts
- Goal setting and tracking
- Working off a to-do list and/or calendar
- Networking/building strong relationships
- Working with a mentor
- Actively saving money (10–20 percent of earnings)
- Waking up early in the morning

Much like good habits, there are many **bad habits** as well. Many of these include:

- Reacting to emails all day
- Wasting time
- Participating in office and personal distractions
- Excessive drinking and/or drug use
- Poor diet
- Thinking negative thoughts
- No daily learning/reading
- Not getting enough quality sleep
- Not regularly exercising
- Being "reactive" in your daily work

Changing habits is not an easy process for most people but if you want a successful career, it is a necessary evil. **Benjamin Franklin said** it best: "Your net worth to *the* world is usually determined *by what* remains after your bad habits *are* subtracted from your good ones."[5] The problem with changing habits resides in how most people poorly go about trying to change them. Think about the 88 percent of us who fail to achieve our New Year's resolutions each year—we make a declaration of objective at the start of each year and then drift back into our bad habits and results.

Many new habits can also be formed as a result of job changes—when most people simply didn't realize how much easier life seemed with their old habits until they were forced to develop new ones with a new organization. Once you leave a company for a new one, there are a whole new set of habit changes that take place, including changes in products, services, cultures, people, location, processes, etc. Because of this, 67 percent of companies recently studied indicate that **it can take seven or more months for a new salesperson to become fully productive after a job change.**[6]

The first step in the process of changing your personal habits is to create a list of your own habits and label them as "good" or "bad." Next you want to eliminate bad habits and start adding good ones. In Tom Corley's book, *Change Your Habits, Change Your Life,* the author suggests documenting everything you habitually do daily from the moment you wake up to when you go to sleep. Next, he suggests eliminating bad habits before adding new ones. Finally, he suggests breaking your habits into three lists: morning, daytime, and nighttime, and slowly changing your habits over a twenty-one day period of time—using a daily checklist of your new habits that you check off each day once completed.

Corley also talks about the two types of habits we have: ordinary habits and keystone habits. Ordinary habits are simple stand-alone habits that only involve one function. Keystone habits, however, are habits that have an impact on other habits—similar to a stack of dominos falling in succession.

An example of a common keystone habit is daily exercise. By simply working out each morning, it could then lead to further changes such as fighting depression, weight loss, higher energy levels and productivity, a better diet, better sleep, lower stress levels, etc. So by working on your keystone habits, you can have a much larger potential impact on all of your habits—similar to a domino effect.

The real power with keystone habits is that one simple habit change can have a multiplier effect. **Common keystone habits typically include:**

- Daily exercise
- Making your bed each morning
- Daily family dinners
- Waking up early in the morning
- Staying organized and planning your day
- Daily goal setting
- Proper time management
- Daily educational reading/learning

Once your habits start to form through daily use and accountability, they will start to become more and more subconscious and second nature to you. How long this takes depends on the complexity of the habit—the more complex, the longer the timeframe. Studies have shown that **the average habit takes around 66 days to fully form in the human brain. More complex habits can take upwards of 90 days.**[7] So the bottom line is that you need to have a plan, set proper expectations, hold yourself accountable daily for your changes, and not give up.

Throughout this book, we will be discussing successful habits that you can develop and use for yourself. Some of these you may already utilize while others may be new to you. The habits I have listed in this book are those that I tend to find the most often in successful salespeople and millionaires today. Just remember that in order to be successful in sales, you have to create your own personal success systems, and these systems are called habits.

# — CHAPTER 4 —

# SUCCESS <u>ALWAYS</u> HAS A NUMBER

• • •

*"Simple can be harder than complex: You have to work hard
to get your thinking clean to make it simple.
But it's worth it in the end because once you get there,
you can move mountains."*
— Steve Jobs

Joe Girard wasn't just any old car salesman. Girard has been recognized by the Guinness Book of World Records as the world's greatest salesman. Over the course of 15 years, Joe sold 13,000 cars. For those not familiar with the automotive sales industry, at the height of his career Joe was selling 18 cars in a single day when the average car salesman sold 5 a month. Joe also gave out 16,000 "uniquely designed" business cards per month when the average salesperson gave out 500 standard ones. Joe gave out $50 referral fees (the equivalent of $200 in 2016) for new-customer referrals when most other salespeople paid nothing. Joe constantly asked for referrals when only 11 percent of salespeople ever do. And most important, Joe learned about and appreciated his clients and wrote each one of them a handwritten, personalized note each month when the average car salesman did not. And what were the results of all these efforts? Nearly 70 percent of Joe's sales came from repeat customers or people they knew.[1]

Like other successful salespeople, Joe had to learn how to become successful. In his early childhood, Joe sold and delivered papers door to door for the *Detroit Free Press*. Joe claimed that it was during this time he "really learned about selling"—especially during their new-subscriber sales contest. The contest was simple: For each new subscriber signed up for at least a month, Joe would win a free case of Pepsi-Cola—which was a big deal to a young kid like Joe at that time. Joe's sales pitch to prospective subscribers was, "We're having a contest, and I'd like you to sign up for just one week." In order for Joe to win, **each new subscriber had to last at least a month, but Joe figured that once they signed up, most of them would not cancel that quickly.**[2]

Joe was so motivated that eventually his garage was lined with free cases of Pepsi-Cola—which he in turn sold to people in his neighborhood, yielding him even more sales and income. Naturally all of this came through hard work and persistence. As Joe explains in his book *How to Sell Anything to Anybody,* "If they [prospective subscribers] said no, I'd keep on going, never giving up, never being disappointed that I didn't keep pushing doorbells." Joe ended up ringing so many doorbells that his "fingers got sore."[3]

But what Joe ended up learning through this process that was so valuable to his future sales career was the law of averages in sales and that success always has a number. The larger the number of doorbells he rang each day the larger the domino effect it had on all of the other goals he wanted to achieve—all starting with the simple push of a button. For Joe knew that each new doorbell rung got him one step closer to:

1. More new potential subscribers, leading to . . .

2. More cases of Pepsi-Cola won, leading to . . .

3. More sales by selling his cases of Pepsi-Cola to neighbors, leading to . . .

4. Higher income and profits, leading to . . .

5. Higher income and productivity per hour worked, leading to . . .

6. Joe one day selling nearly eighteen cars in a single day, leading to . . .

7. Joe ultimately being recognized by the Guinness Book of World Records as the world's greatest salesman.

All of this started with one simple action: ringing enough doorbells every day. **This simple yet all-important action became the "keystone" to Joe's success** and a lesson that served him well throughout his world-record career in sales. In the end, all salespeople, like Joe, will succeed or fail based on their own "keystone" sales activities. And ALL keystones have one thing in common: They are all managed by a number.

## KNOW THE SIMPLE SALES EQUATION

Success and failure in sales all comes down to a very simple yet powerful equation: **ACTIVITY x EFFECTIVENESS = RESULTS.** In order to succeed in sales, you need to have a firm grasp of this equation and use it as a lens through which you measure your progress. Let's briefly look at each component of this equation:

**Activity** is nothing more than the actions you and your supporting resources do to help you in your everyday sales work. Activity is typically measured by the quantity of your actions, such as the total number of phone calls, appointments, sales closed, etc., in a finite period of time. Higher levels of activity typically come from salespeople who are highly engaged in their work, well motivated, and working from a sales activity plan. For most sales professionals, activity is frequently highest during their early stages with a new organization. In the story of young Joe Girard, all activity started with the ringing of doorbells.

**Effectiveness** is how impactful your activities become, and is measured by the "quality" of your work. Most seasoned salespeople will tell you that with experience comes higher levels of effectiveness, which is often reflected in higher close rates, average order sizes, call conversions, and new engagements. If you are new to selling specific products, services, industries, and organizations, your initial levels of effectiveness will typically be lower due to a lack of experience. Conversely, if this is a role you are familiar with in your previous work, then your levels of effectiveness should be higher. Again, young Joe Girard became more effective by doing things like asking subscribers to sign up for only a week, knowing it would produce higher close rates and better overall results.

**Results** are nothing more than what you end up producing as a result of your activities and effectiveness. Results are commonly measured in sales, meetings, close rates, etc.

# The Simple Sales Equation

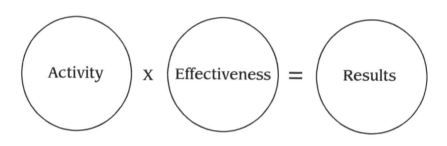

| Marketing | How many new high quality sales leads are you able to produce and at what Cost-Per-Lead (CPL) | Enough sales leads generated to convert and support defined sales objectives and achieve the highest Return-On-Investment (ROI) |
|---|---|---|
| Prospecting | How many new sales eads are you able to move into your defined sales process? | Higher lead conversion rates |
| Customer Qualification | How well do you identify each customer's unique goals and gaps to sell to? | Higher lead qualification rates |
| Presentation /Positioning | How well do you present and convey a high value exchange to each sales prospect | Higher prospect conversions and average order values |
| Sales Objections/ Delays | Ability to overcome objections and move a sale out of a "Stall" | Faster sales velocity and average sales cycle time |
| Closing | Total opportunities closed | Higher closing ratios |

| Asking For Referrals | Habitually and successfully ask for referrals from the "Right" people at the "Right" times | Higher customer referral business based on referral lead source |
|---|---|---|
| Generating Repeat Business | Successfully "Stay in Front" of former and current customers | Higher customer retention rates, reorders, and life-time customer value to the business |

In sales, you cannot have activity without effectiveness and vice versa—anything times zero always results in a zero. For example, without activity, there would be no sales since you would have nobody to sell to—no matter how effective you are. Conversely, you may be able to fill your day with sales activities and meetings, but if you lack the effectiveness to sell and close during those meetings, you will have no results.

This equation is also helpful based on the tenure of most salespeople. Most salespeople just starting out are typically highly engaged due to a higher level of initial excitement over their new roles, which means they are well motivated to operate at a level of high activity. However, since they are newer and learning, their effectiveness levels may be lower and therefore they need a higher level of activity (calls, meetings, etc.) to compensate for their lower level of effectiveness (close ratios, call conversions, etc.) to make their sales objectives.

For more tenured sales professionals, it is not uncommon to see higher levels of sales effectiveness due to experience combined with lower levels of activity. Many senior salespeople will intuitively act upon this sales equation by intentionally lowering their levels of activity and compensating for this through a higher level of effectiveness in their activities. For example, a new salesperson may have a close ratio of 20 percent, meaning he/she needs five meetings to close every one sale. An experienced salesperson, through increased sales effectiveness, may have developed a 50 percent close ratio, meaning he/she will only need two meetings to close a sale versus five for the newer salesperson.

Top sales professionals are unique because they will commonly maintain high levels of both activity and effectiveness, knowing that the two are intertwined and paramount to their success. They also know that even though higher effectiveness can be a substitute for lower activity, both must be constantly improved upon to achieve maximum sales results.

The most fundamental mistake many sales professionals make is in the understanding of capacity in both their activity and effectiveness. **Unlike activity, sales effectiveness is unique since it is limitless in application.** With activity, you and your supporting resources have a finite level of capacity—commonly measured in time. Most sales professionals only have around 2,350 working hours in any year. Effectiveness, on the other hand, is potentially limitless and infinite, which is why it is commonly the deciding factor between the failing 87 percent and the top 13 percent of professionals in selling and results.

Due to its unlimited scalability, sales effectiveness is something every sales professional needs to learn through experience, training, and self-learning. The fact that you are reading this book is a good indication of the direction you're taking here. The bottom line is that nearly all salespeople sell without a college degree in selling. Therefore, you need to constantly learn and get better—especially at the one thing that is unlimited in your sales work: your sales effectiveness. If you can accomplish that while consistently maintaining a high level of sales activity, you will be far ahead of most of your peers today.

## KNOW YOUR KEYSTONE SALES NUMBERS

**The best way to reach any sales goal is to break it down into daily activities.** Without a daily focus, salespeople are left with weekly, monthly, quarterly, and annual measurements that in most cases are too difficult to effectively measure and manage—especially when it becomes too late to do anything about it. This is why you as a sales professional need to take this upon yourself.

In order to make this work, you need to start with the math. Most people will work around 46 weeks a year when excluding holidays, vacations, sick time, etc. This works out to around **230 working days in a year.** Once you have defined your annual sales goal/s for the year, take that number and divide it by 230, which will give you your daily goal/s.

For example, let's say your goal is to close $500,000 in new sales (business) this year. If you know your average sale size/client revenue ($4,000), your average call-to-meeting success rate (10 percent), and your average sales-meeting close rate (20 percent), you can then quickly determine your daily goals based on the following equations:

- **Daily Sales Goal:**
  $500,000/230 = **$2,174/day** (Annual sales target/230 days)

- **Daily Sales Meetings:**
  [($500,000/($4,000 X 20 percent)/230] = **2.7 meetings/day**
  [(Annual sales target/(Average Sale Size X Average Close Rate)/230]

- **Daily Sales Calls:**
  2.7/10 percent = **27 sales calls/day**
  (Daily Sales Meetings/Average Call-to-Meeting Success Rate)

These "daily" sales activity numbers now become your "keystone sales numbers" since they are those things you must complete each day in order to achieve all of your other sales objectives moving forward. Based on the calculation above, you know you would have **one keystone sales number (27 sales calls per day)** that once completed will ultimately lead you to all of your other sales objectives — all things being equal, of course. If the other variables, such as your call-to-meeting conversion rate, average order size, and sales close rate change, all you need to do is rerun your calculations to get back to your keystone sales number.

Many salespeople may have more than one keystone number (calls, drop-ins, emails, etc.), so make sure to calculate them all based on the same equations above. For example, I had a top-performing salesperson who set a goal of visiting each potential sales prospect in his territory at least once a year. His territory had around 1,350 prospects, so by dividing that number by 230 workdays in a year, he had his keystone number of at least six drop-ins per day (1,350 prospects/230 working days). Since this number was typically twice the average rate of his peers, his sales numbers were typically twice as high in comparison.

For those professionals with much longer sales cycles and/or very high average sales sizes, using a daily sales activity plan may not seem practical, which is okay. The most important point to remember here is what DAILY ACTIVITIES you need to engage in to achieve your sales goals whenever the sale takes place. For example, a typical sale may take a few months to close and therefore cannot be tracked down to daily sales activities. But by equating your sales numbers down to a daily average, you can then derive what your daily keystone sales numbers are for your sales activities needed to hit your monthly goal—which is your primary focus here. If the numbers don't end up working out in your sales targets, then you need to make adjustments to your other sales activities that support it.

Just remember: **There are four to five major elements you need to know in order to actually develop and refine your keystone numbers for any activity.** These include:

1. Your annual sales objective $_____

2. Days worked per year (typically 230)

3. Your average order size $_____

4. Your average contact-to-sales-meeting ratio (if your activity is to set up a sales meeting)_____%

5. Your average close ratio (from either your contact or your sales meeting)_____%

Once you have established all of your daily keystone sales numbers, you now have the basis for your daily sales activity planner, which will be used to put your keystone numbers into daily action.

# FOLLOW A DAILY SALES ACTIVITY CHECKLIST

Ryan was one of the best salespeople I'd ever worked with and had just completed his best sales month with the company. We affectionately nicknamed Ryan "The Machine" because he never stopped and worked his tail off each and every day. During our November sales meeting, I told everybody what Ryan had previously told me just before the beginning of October.

"October is going to be my best sales month ever," said Ryan.

When I asked Ryan why he thought this, his response was that he had a ton of opportunities in the pipeline ready to close in October.

Well, October passed and Ryan did in fact have the best sales month with the company. During the sales meeting that followed, I asked Ryan how many of those pipeline opportunities he was so excited about heading into October had actually closed. His response to the group: "Zero!"

Ryan's story illustrates a number of critical lessons about selling — the most significant of which is **the importance of maintaining daily keystone sales activities no matter what your pipeline looks like.** In many industries, sales can be a highly unpredictable process, and the worst mistake many poor-performing salespeople will make is forgoing their daily activities in the hopes that what they project to close will in fact close that month. Salespeople who do this clearly lack the discipline, focus, and the daily habits needed to prevent this from happening. That is where a sales daily activity checklist can help.

In the previous section we discussed how to calculate and identify your daily keystone activities for success. Now it's time to put them into action. One of the most effective ways I have found to do this is to create a simple one-page "Daily Activity Checklist" (see example below). And here's how it works.

Prior to each month, print off enough copies for each workday of the month and place them on your desk. Every morning, pick up a new sheet, date it, and do not finish your workday until AFTER all of your daily activities are completed and checked off your list. There are a number of benefits to using this list, including:

- It allows you to modify your keystone activities as needed based on the needs and performance levels you calculate and track over time. Because of this, I suggest creating a copy in a word processing document and modifying as needed.

- It creates a minimum level of daily keystone activities that must be completed to hit your overall sales objectives—no matter how long it takes your sales cycle to close.

- It helps provide you with the will and focus for your workdays, and helps remove lower-priority distractions that can take valuable sales activity time away from you as they occur.

- It holds YOU personally accountable to yourself for your own performance and provides a tool to reflect on what you have accomplished at the end of each and every workday.

DAILY ACTIVITY CHECKLIST
(EXAMPLE–MODIFY AS NEEDED)


Date: _____

SALES ACTIVITIES:
❏ 2–3 sales meetings (new clients)
❏ 1–2 sales meetings (existing clients)
❏ Daily breakfast and/or lunch sales meeting

PROSPECTING ACTIVITIES:
❏ Cold Call 60–100 new sales prospects
❏ Drop in 6–8 new sales prospects (in area of daily appointments)
❏ Email 20–30 new sales prospects
❏ Schedule lunch/breakfast sales/referral meetings for the next day/s
❏ Make 25 follow-up calls on active opportunities and previous prospects
❏ Schedule at least 3–4 additional new appointments
❏ Map out your sales meetings and drop-in locations for next day

Weekly Close Targets: 1–3 sales (list targets below):


❏ _____ Mtg Date:_____


❏ _____ Mtg Date:_____


❏ _____ Mtg Date:_____

# — CHAPTER 5 —

# PERSONAL GOALS — SETTING YOUR PATH TO SUCCESS

• • •

*"The difference between a successful person*
*and others is not a lack of strength,*
*not a lack of knowledge, but rather a lack of will."*
*— Vince Lombardi*

One of the first salespeople I ever worked with when I got into sales was Eric. He was by far the most successful salesperson at his company for a number of years and I took notes and tried to observe everything he was doing to be successful. What was so remarkable about Eric wasn't how he managed his clients and sales but rather his laser-focus on his simple goals written at the base of his computer screen every day. When I first noticed this, I started to ask him questions.

"Eric, I notice every morning you have two numbers written below your computer screen," I said. "One changes every day while the other changes each month. Nobody else has these on their computers, so I wanted to ask you why you do."

Eric looked up with a smile and said, "Dustin, in order to be successful in sales here you need to be laser-focused. Do you ever notice what I do when everybody wants to chat in their cubes and waste time online?"

"Yeah, you just keep your head down and seem to ignore it all," I responded.

"And how about all those non-essential meetings that you never see me attend?" said Eric.

"I never see you there, either," I responded with a chuckle.

"Exactly," responded Eric. "I am here for one simple reason, Dustin, and that is to hit my goals that are written on the bottom of my PC every day. The number on the left is my daily sales number and the one on the right is my monthly sales goal. If I don't hit those numbers each and every day, I won't make the money I need to support my family, I won't make it to President's Club each year with my wife, I won't be able to win all the sales awards I win every year, and I won't be able to move forward in my career. All of these things come down to those two simple numbers on my screen, and as long as I don't lose that focus, I will never fail. They're written on my PC for a reason: I stare at them and they stare right back at me all day, reminding me to not lose focus and to always keep my eye on the ball."

If there's one common thread among nearly all highly successful people in sales and in life, it is a path to success defined by a goal. Top-performing salespeople know what success means to them by defining that success in a goal and working tirelessly to achieve it. And it is not just salespeople who benefit from this habit. Fully **80 percent of self-made millionaires have indicated that they not only set and lived by goals, but they were obsessed by pursuing them.**[1]

Harvard University did a study of their 1979 graduates and found that 10 years after their graduation, there was a significant variation in incomes between those who had goals and those who did not. In their findings, 84 percent of their graduates indicated they had no goals established, 13 percent had goals that were not in writing, and 3 percent had written goals. For the 13 percent who had goals that were not in writing, they earned on average twice as much as the 84 percent with no goals. For the 3 percent who had written goals, they earned 10 times as much income as the other 97 percent combined.[2]

**As a sales professional, the greatest advantage goals provide you with is focus.** The top sales performers want to achieve great results, and the best way to accomplish this is by defining goals and staying laser-focused on them. When creating good sales goals, remember that they should be reasonable, achievable, written, executable, and mutually agreed upon by all involved.

In developing a laser-focus on defined goals, successful sales professionals are not only able to focus in on what they want, but they are also able to effectively remove all of the competing priorities and obstacles that potentially stand in the way. Author Greg McKeown wrote that focus is "not just haphazardly saying no [to distractions], but purposefully, deliberately, and strategically eliminating the nonessentials. Not just once a year as part of a planning meeting, but constantly reducing, focusing, and simplifying. Not just getting rid of the obvious time wasters, but being willing to cut out really terrific opportunities as well. Few appear to have the courage to live this principle, which may be why it differentiates successful people and organizations from the very successful ones."[3]

Failing sales professionals treat sales-goal setting in a similar manner to how the 88 percent of us treat a New Year's resolution—we make a declaration of an objective at the start of each year and then drift back into our bad habits and results as time passes by. The primary reason for this failure is a lack of personal accountability. **A goal without accountability is nothing more than a dream.** Most sales professionals today will commonly create their annual goals and then never follow up on them with good habits throughout the course of the year.

When it comes to sales professionals, it is important to understand that inspiration and desire is what may have gotten you started in your career, but is it **your habits that will keep you going and continue to make you successful.** Habits are inherently no different than business systems, since habits are systems you create for yourself. Just as you cannot run and scale a business without systems, you equally cannot grow your own productivity without good habits.

## LEARN THROUGH REFLECTION

As children, many of us either had a hamster or knew others who did. What was so unique and entertaining about the hamster was its habitual marathon running along a hamster wheel. We all would amusingly watch as the hamster, free of any real cognitive reasoning, willfully jumped onto a hamster wheel and ran and ran and ran. Why? What is it that compels a hamster to want to run on a wheel until exhausted, and where does he think he's going? More important, are you as a sales professional guilty of the same kind of problem?

Most sales professionals jump onto the proverbial hamster wheel each day, work until they are exhausted, and do it all over again—day after day, month after month, year after year. Was this your dream when you decided to become a sales professional? And how is what you're doing now any different than what the hamster does on his wheel? You may be getting paid, but most sales professionals who don't truly know the value of their time end up working longer hours for less pay per hour. At least the hamster can get off the wheel when he wants to—most sales professionals cannot.

The main difference between a hamster and a human is the human's ability to learn. And **learning can only come through reflection. Many of the most successful businesspeople I've met in my life had an unusually strong sense of reflection**. These people typically viewed unfavorable outcomes as another opportunity to learn and grow. To them, failure was only the result of the inability to learn, adjust, and move on. In short, they are able to see the hamster wheel for what it really is. Their ability to adhere to this mindset comes largely from a keen and habitual sense of reflection.

Reflection commonly takes place daily, weekly, monthly, and yearly for most successful people. They realize, intentionally or not, that reflection is needed to pull one's psyche out of the hamster wheel of their daily lives and learn and reflect from a basis of "why."

To help illustrate this point, I often tell sales professionals to start the first step of this process by writing down their accomplishments on a whiteboard or piece of paper at the end of each day and reviewing it when the workday is done—with no further distractions. I then notice what happens to them both psychologically and physically when they realize just how much they have actually accomplished in their workday; or better yet, what have they forgotten they accomplished and are now having a hard time recalling? Without daily reflection, most sales professionals don't realize this and often leave their days feeling like they accomplished little and with little purpose.

The next step in reflection is to start your days by writing down your goals for the coming day, executing on those goals, and then reflecting on your goals before your day is done. Goals now allow you to create focus for your reflection. One of the reasons I recommend sales professionals create a daily goals checklist is to give them a daily basis of defined goals and a means to reflect on them.

When you begin your reflection process, do it chronologically, as if you are rewinding your day all over again. Walk through what happened, what you learned from it, what you could do differently next time, and what you ultimately accomplished. **Remember, good reflection relies on focus, focus comes from goals, goals support your purpose, and ALL are executed through good habits.**

Once you begin your new journey into reflection, make sure to stop by a pet store and buy a hamster wheel. Place it on your desk and use it as a visual aid when you start your daily reflection process. This will serve as a reminder that you will never again work without clear direction, focus, purpose, and vision—all aided by your learning through reflection.

# — CHAPTER 6 —

# STOP WASTING YOUR TIME!

• • •

*"A man who dares to waste one hour of time*
*has not discovered the value of life.."*
*— Charles Darwin*

"If only I had more time in the day" were the first words out of Linda's mouth when I asked her how she plans her days. This is not the first time I've heard this statement from a salesperson and unfortunately won't be the last.

"Linda, why do you think you need more time in your day to be more successful?" I asked.

"I just can't seem to get enough sales in each day," Linda replied with an exhausted look on her face.

"And how does that make you feel?" I asked.

"Terrible . . . like I am failing," replied Linda. "I'm working harder than I ever have but it seems like despite all my efforts I'm not hitting quota and my sales clearly show that. It seems like there are simply not enough hours in the day and I don't want to waste them. You know the old saying, Dustin: 'Time is money.'"

Anybody who tells you that "time is money" has not figured out that only money can be re-earned—time cannot. Every day we can make thousands of choices—both good and bad—with our time and money, but at the end of the day, only one always runs out.

Most people fail at time management because they simply don't know what their time is potentially worth to them. Instead, they let others manage their time for them and then they get "paid" in exchange for their time. In the end, most salespeople today are in the same business: trading their time for money.

In order to become successful in business, you need to understand a key fundamental of business: namely, what you and others are worth in time. Each resource in business, including yourself, is limited by time and/or cost. You can only work so many hours in a day, week, month, and year, and then you run out of time and the ability to create more of it on your own.

In order to better understand the value of time we need to start with the numbers. When it comes to salespeople, here is where I typically begin. First, the most important resource you have in sales is your time. There are 365 days in a year, which means you have 8,760 total hours to work with for everything in your life. Of the 52 weeks you have to work with, most sales professionals will be down to 47 weeks of work after holidays, vacations, sick time, and time away from work, leaving you with **2,350 hours** to work with based on a 10-hour workday.

Now let's set a financial goal: What do you want/need to earn this year to be successful? In Linda's case, her stated goal is to earn $200,000 this year before income taxes. Dividing her desired income ($200,000) by her total hours worked (2,350) gives her a cost per hour ($85). Now Linda knows what the cost for her time on an hourly basis ($85) should be.

| HOW TO CALCULATE THE VALUE OF YOUR TIME DURING WORKING HOURS | | |
|---|---|---|
| Your Targeted Annual Income | Average Annual Hours Worked | Your Cost Per Hour |
| $50,000 | 2,350 | $21 |
| $100,000 | 2,350 | $43 |
| $150,000 | 2,350 | $64 |
| $200,000 | 2,350 | $85 |
| $250,000 | 2,350 | $106 |
| $300,000 | 2,350 | $128 |
| $400,000 | 2,350 | $170 |
| $500,000 | 2,350 | $213 |
| $600,000 | 2,350 | $255 |
| $700,000 | 2,350 | $298 |
| $800,000 | 2,350 | $340 |

"So what you're telling me is that my time is really worth $85 an hour?" asked Linda.

"Your time is worth as much or as little as you want it to be worth," I replied. "If your goal is to earn $200,000 this year, then that is what your time is worth at that goal."

"But what if I want to one day be like your other employee, Ryan, and work four days a week so I can have an extra day with my children?" asked Linda.

"Simple," I replied. "Remove those workdays (47) and hours (470) from the previous total hours worked (2,350), which leaves you with a new total of 1,880 hours of work for the year. Based on your sales goal of $200,000, that leaves you with a new price per hour of $107 ($200,000 / 1,880)."

"But what if I can't earn that much money per hour?" asked Linda. "I already told you that I was too busy as it is."

"Your problem is not that you're too busy, Linda," I replied. "Your problem is that you are not productive with your time. There are a number of ways you can start fixing this problem, starting today."

## STAYING BUSY VERSUS STAYING PRODUCTIVE

**There is a big difference between staying busy and staying productive.** Staying busy is a time killer because it is statically tied to the limited resource of time. Productivity, on the other hand, allows you to increase your output (sales) based on the same amount of limited resources (time). Most salespeople today spend the majority of their time in "NON-SELLING" activities. Recent studies have shown that salespeople spend as little at 41 percent of their time actually selling, which means that most salespeople are spending nearly 59 percent of their time *not* selling.[1]

If you want to continue to grow your sales, you need to think about everything you do in terms of productivity. Some of the most common ways you can help improve your own sales productivity include:

- Strategically scheduling your daily sales meetings and prospecting in the same geographic areas. Always have a backup plan when schedules suddenly change so you limit time wasted moving from point A to point B and so forth.

- Staying HIGHLY organized during your workday.

- Removing all distractions (TV, gossip, browsing the Internet, social media, etc.) that take you away from your daily sales goals. For example, studies about TV watching alone have shown that 77 percent of "poor" people watch more than an hour of TV a day versus 67 percent of self-made millionaires who watch less than an hour.[2]

- Planning your days in advance and using a to-do list for those items that can wait and be done during non-selling hours.

- Using sales productivity (CRM) systems to help better manage your time, resources, and follow-ups.

- Hiring appointment setters and/or administrative assistants to handle more of your non-sales related activities.

- Constantly reading, training, and learning about new ways to make yourself better.

- Not participating in time-wasting meetings without a clearly defined agenda and purpose.

- If you work from a home office, make sure that it is 100 percent designated as a work-only space without personal distractions and interruptions during work hours.

If you happen to find yourself feeling "too busy" like Linda, it is best to start asking yourself why you feel this way and then start taking steps to improve your productivity to address this problem. Productivity improvements start with you first, but certainly shouldn't end there. There are other ways—and people—you can use to help improve your own productivity as well.

## BUYING TIME FROM OTHERS

Linda is like many struggling salespeople who feel like they are simply running out of time. After she improves her own time productivity, she can then consider buying the time of others. In the example above, Linda's ultimate desired cost of her working time is $107 per hour. So what can Linda buy now at an hourly rate that costs less than what she costs? The reality is she can buy a lot! Entry-level labor in most markets today can start at $8–$15 per hour—significantly less than what her time is worth. Recent government data also shows that the cost of a receptionist alone in the US today is only around $13 per hour.[3]

There is a reason why businesses grow by scaling their labor force, and Linda should be no different. Rome was not built in a day and it certainly wasn't built alone. I frequently remind people in business that Bill Gates became a billionaire by creating a lot of millionaires. The point is that in order to succeed, grow, and be happy, you will need help. So how does Linda make this happen?

Now that Linda knows what her time is potentially worth, she can start writing down all of her daily sales activities in detail. The most precise way to do this is to clock herself on each of these tasks and/or the resources she utilizes to complete them for a whole day. This can involve everything from sales meetings, scheduling, prospecting, marketing, phone calls, emails, proposal creation, order processing, data entry, trade shows, reporting, commuting, etc. Anything that takes time to complete should be documented for consideration.

Next, once Linda has all of her time functions written down, she can answer the following questions:

- Which functions can only be completed by Linda (or you) and nobody else? What is the total amount of time allocated to those functions?

- Which functions could be completed by somebody else in support of Linda (or you)? What is the total amount time allocated to those functions?

- Of those functions that can be completed by somebody other than Linda (or you), what type of person/s would need to be hired to complete them and at what cost per hour?

The ultimate goal for Linda is to get as many low-cost, low-return, and time-consuming activities off her plate as possible. If these tasks can be successfully completed by anybody who charges less than $107 per hour, then Linda's first objective should be to get these activities procedurally documented and in the hands of these people as quickly as possible. The time needed for Linda to create a step-by-step procedure for any or all of these activities can be time intensive at first but well worth it in the long run—especially when it comes to dealing with turnover, which you can expect to be higher at lower hourly price ranges.

The benefit to getting as many lower-cost activities off Linda's plate and into the hands of lower-cost labor is twofold. Not only will she be able to lower her time-cost per activity, but she will also be able to free up more of her time for those functions that provide the highest return. Namely, more sales meetings.

Let's do the math. Say Linda identifies five hours (50 percent) of her daily tasks that could be supported by other people. If Linda pays them $15 per hour to complete them all, Linda's total support cost would come to only $75 per day. If Linda can now reallocate those extra five hours to more sales meeting activity, she could then increase her productivity by up to $460 ($535 in new sales – $75 in labor-support costs) per day. Over the course of a year, this could result in a net new productivity gain of $86,480 in new sales income per year! All obtained by doing nothing more than buying other people's time. In short, around 43 percent of Linda's desired annual income target could now be achieved through the productivity gains received from buying other people's time alone!

| DAILY TASK REASSIGNMENT LIST (EXAMPLE) | | | | | |
|---|---|---|---|---|---|
| Activity | Time (hours) | Can be Completed by Support? | Support Needed | Support Cost per Hour | Support Cost per Day |
| Scheduling | 0.4 | Yes | Assistant | $13.00 | $5.20 |
| Cold Calling | 1.6 | Yes | Appointment Setter | $16.00 | $25.60 |
| Proposal Creation | 0.7 | Yes | Assistant | $13.00 | $9.10 |
| Email Prospecting | 1 | Yes | Appointment Setter | $16.00 | $16.00 |
| Order Processing | 0.3 | Yes | Assistant | $13.00 | $3.90 |
| CRM Data Entry | 0.5 | Yes | Assistant | $13.00 | $6.50 |
| Follow-upCalls | 0.5 | Yes | Appointment Setter | $16.00 | $8.00 |
| Commuting | 1 | No | NA | NA | NA |
| Sales Meetings | 3 | No | NA | NA | NA |
| Lunch Meetings | 1 | No | NA | NA | NA |
| Totals: | 10 | | | | $74.30 |

The potential resources needed to help support you in this process can typically come from many different places ranging from local job boards such as Craigslist to even your own networks and connections. I once had a salesperson who worked as a team with his spouse. During the days he would rapidly move from one sales meeting to another while his spouse ran all of the operations in the background, ranging from managing his calendar, contracts, order processing, follow-up, prospecting, etc. As a result, they both realized that the incremental revenue they received through his productivity gains by working together were actually greater than what her previous job was paying her. So she wisely decided to quit her old job so they could collectively earn more money by working together.

Once Linda has all of her activities well identified, timed-out, and written down for others to complete on her behalf, she will also be able to more effectively hire and manage the people and resources needed to run them on a more consistent basis moving forward. Since your systems will now run these processes, it becomes far less important who she hires and when they may need replacing since the documented processes she created will always remain with her. More important, she will also know the real value of each employee, including herself, and how best to align the resources to their appropriate levels of productivity.

## JOIN THE 5 A.M. CLUB

*"Early to bed and early to rise makes a man healthy, wealthy, and wise."*
*—Benjamin Franklin*

I met Robert during his last tour of duty in the Middle East. Robert was a member of the US Special Forces and part of an elite team fighting battles that most of us will never learn of in places most of us have never heard of. People like Robert are the "silent warriors" who show me time and again why freedom is never free. Robert is one of my heroes.

When I first met Robert, I would occasionally go running with him and his team—that is if I was able to make it out the door by 5:10 a.m.

to join them. Their daily routines (and habits) were to rise early, always make their beds, and go for a run—all before 6 a.m.

When people like Robert start out in their military careers, boot camp is their first habitual indoctrination to waking up at 5 a.m. sharp. At first, some soldiers will struggle developing this new habit but many will tell you that around week four, this becomes more natural and normal. In other words, their brains will have now been programmed to this new habit.

I recently reconnected with Robert to get caught up on our lives. Many years had passed since we first met and he and his team had either moved on from the military or were now retired. Robert had successfully moved on to his new career, and I thought I would give him a call since I happened to be in town.

"Hey, Robert; it's Dustin Ruge," I said over the phone.

"Hey, Dustin! Wow, it's been a while, hasn't it?" replied Robert.

"Too long," I said. "I'm in your neck of the woods this week on business and would like to get together if we can."

"Sure. How about breakfast Wednesday morning?" asked Robert. "Does 6 a.m. work for you?"

"6 a.m.?!" I replied with a chuckle. "Did you go back into the military or something?" Now, I must admit, I am not what most people would consider to be an early-morning person. That is why I've always admired people like Robert, who are.

"Nope, it's just a good habit I never got rid of," replied Robert.

On Wednesday morning I met Robert for breakfast—at 6 a.m. sharp. Not to my surprise, Robert arrived early—go figure. During the course of our conversations I asked him again about his habit of getting up at 5 a.m. every morning—many years after he left military life.

"Robert, it's been over 15 years since we first met and you are still up every morning at 5 a.m.?" I asked. "What does your wife think about all that?" I asked with a smile.

"She wants me to be successful and knows that is where it all begins for me every day," replied Robert.

"Just out of curiosity, how many of your former team members are still doing the same thing?" I asked.

Robert slowly sat back in his chair and with a smile on his face replied, "Only the successful ones."

Recent studies of self-made millionaires found that around 44 percent of them **wake up at least three hours BEFORE their normal workday begins.**[4] Much like Robert, many early risers attribute a great deal of their success to this simple habit. Moreover, this habit is perhaps the strongest keystone habit since it helps start the domino effect leading to many other good habits throughout your day.

As previously discussed, time is limited and as such is a zero-sum game whereby time spent on one activity is time taken away from another. Successful people also know that certain times are better times than others—especially when it comes to spending time wisely. For example, if it takes you 45 minutes to commute in heavy traffic to work at 7 a.m. versus 20 minutes if you leave at 6 a.m., what value is that extra 25 minutes to your life and your day? Successful people highly value time and find ways to not waste it.

Another benefit of starting your day early is the ability to get the brain going for maximum results when the workday actually begins. Recent studies show that the human brain is sharpest two to four hours after waking. So if you start your day at 5 a.m., this means that your brain should be to the point of maximum performance when the workday starts at 8 a.m. for everybody else.[5]

Because of this heightened level of brain productivity and energy at the start of your workdays, make sure you schedule your most important sales activities first—especially those that require higher levels of creativity. Energy levels tends to wane later on in the day for many of us, so try to schedule more of your "busy" work and internal meetings for later in the day to better match your energy levels.

The following are some of the biggest advantages to joining the 5 a.m. Club. Many will claim that there are more that could be added to this list, but these are the ones I tend see the most:

- **Time to exercise**—Most gyms open very early in the morning and the earlier you arrive, the less time you will need to wait for a machine to open up in a normally busy gym. Exercising in the morning also helps to produce an increased flow of endorphins and dopamine to the brain, resulting in higher levels of energy and positive emotions in most people, which can last throughout the workday. Studies have also shown that after a stressful day at work people are less likely to want to exercise and more likely to procrastinate and watch TV. In short, exercising in the mornings helps get your body and your day going strong.[6]

- **Time to educationally read**—Many people who don't start their days early will complain about not having enough "alone time" in their lives. Our minds are wired to learn, and by reading early, our brains release dopamine and serotonin to help grow more brain cells and increase our level of happiness for the day ahead. By starting your day early, you afford yourself more alone time to read and find better balance in your life.

- **Time to make your own time**—How much time is really something you can call "your own time" anymore? If you have a family and work, you are likely being constantly pulled in all directions. Waking up before all of these distractions start can give you peace of mind and the time to help "balance" yourself moving forward.

- **Time not wasted commuting**—The average American today spends around 26 minutes commuting to and from work each day.[7] In many heavy-traffic cities like New York, Los Angeles, Atlanta, etc., commuting can take hours away from your day. Most people commute during times called "rush hours," when it seems like everybody is out commuting at the same time and clogging up the streets. By getting up early, you can save those precious minutes and hours each day simply by beating the rush.

- **Time to plan and get a head start on the day ahead**—Let's face it: The world is increasingly full of distractions and most of them start after 8:00 each morning. Planning and starting your day before the chaos begins is the easiest way to help remove those distractions and get things done.

- **Time to follow and pursue your own dreams**—We all have responsibilities that we need to work for and support during the day, but what about your own dreams? When do you make time for them? As a young child, Warren Buffett delivered newspapers for the *Washington Post*. During that time, Warren ran multiple routes delivering what he estimated to be around 500,000 news-papers, earning a penny each. That $5,000 in earnings would later became the seed money for the financial empire he would eventually build, and was earned in the very early mornings before he went to school.[8]

## REMOVE DISTRACTIONS

I opened a fortune cookie during my sophomore year of college and the fortune inside read, "Procrastination is the thief of time." Now, whoever decided to put that fortune in a college student's fortune cookie must have been brilliant at market segmentation, because I taped that fortune to the top of my TV set—and there it stayed for over a decade.

If procrastination is the thief of time, then distractions are the enabler of procrastination. As previously indicated, time is a zero-sum game whereby time spent on one activity is time taken away from another. Studies have shown that we tend to procrastinate when the activities we do are considered to be boring, difficult, frustrating, lacking in clear meaning and/or reward, or seem unstructured.[9]

THERE ARE ONLY TWO WAYS YOU CAN MANAGE YOUR LIMITED WORKING TIME

TIME EARNING

TIME WASTING

In order to help overcome distractions leading to procrastination and poor sales performance, there are a few key steps you can start taking now. These include:

- Disconnect from the Internet, mobile, and social media world when you have something that needs to get done. Arguably the greatest total waste of time nearly all of us face today is online and on our mobile devices—especially since the vast majority of our time online is spent procrastinating. Our smart phones are now with us everywhere and many of us have literally programed our minds to immediately put our heads down into our mobile devices at any time—especially when we want to procrastinate. The challenge today is that many of our jobs rely on this connectivity, which makes it even harder to simply "disconnect" while working. In the perfect world we would all have a separate PC and mobile device dedicated to work and programmed to be devoid of many of these disruptive functions. But most of us don't live in that world. That means that we all need to hold ourselves accountable and keep track of our wasted time so we can take actions and focus away from it. Psychologists say that the first step in solving a problem is admitting it exists. For most of us, this should be a simple admission. Daily activity checklists and accountability are two of the best ways to help tame this problem for salespeople.

- Work off of a daily activity checklist and hold yourself accountable. Writing down a daily, standard set of goals and then executing on those goals each day is critical to creating consistency and focus in performance. Daily checklists also allow for reflection on your progress before your day is done so you can hold yourself accountable and help remove the temptation of distractions. One of the reasons I recommend salespeople create a daily activity checklist is to give them a daily basis of defined goals and a means to reflect on them.

- Do not react to emails. How much time would you guess you spend each week checking your emails? Recent studies have shown that the average worker now spends around 30 hours a week checking emails—and that doesn't even include the additional time for managing and responding to them![10] Think about that: If you are working 10-hour days and 50 hours a week, over 60 percent of your time could be spent just handling emails! If you want to stop wasting your time, this is one of the best places to start. I always recommend that salespeople check their email only three times a day: at 10 a.m., 1 p.m., and 5 p.m. If people become concerned that you are not getting back to them quickly enough, create an auto-responder for every email received indicating exactly when you check emails each day and when they can expect a response from you. This solves most problems surrounding scheduled email time frames.

- Turn off notifications on your PC and smart phones. Think about all of the technological disruptions you receive each day. Do you see an Outlook alert each time you receive a new email? Do your apps "ping" you when something new happens on your smart phone? How about notifications from your smart phone every time a new text arrives? Do your friends on social media sites interrupt your day through their own update alerts? The trick is to turn all notifications OFF during working hours—period! This includes on your smart phone, your PC, etc.

- Set time limits on activities and work off of a calendar. Have you ever felt like you mentally "hit a wall" doing something for too long? We all have. One of the easiest ways to lose focus is to have too much time to simply finish a task and move on. For this reason, set limits on your time devoted to tasks, thereby creating a deadline and further reason to focus on completing the task at hand.

- Take "time-outs" in your days. Studies have shown that taking short breaks (five minutes) while working helps with memory retention and improving focus.[11] In grade school, we would commonly take a few "recesses" each day, which helped us break up the day, improve focus, and learn. What exactly did working organizations not learn about the benefits of periodic breaks that we did growing up?

## THE BEST DEFENSE IS A GOOD OFFENSE— SCHEDULE YOUR DAYS IN ADVANCE

One of the differences I consistently see between successful and failing salespeople has to do with how they plan for and manage their days. Successful salespeople will commonly play offense by having a detailed plan for each hour of each workday while failing salespeople will not. Anybody who follows American football knows that it is very hard to consistently move the ball and score if your defense is always stuck on the field. Top salespeople know this as well.

There are **three** primary tools use can use to help successfully manage your days and make the most of your time:

**Daily Activity Checklist.** A daily activity checklist is nothing more than a one-page list of standard to-do items that you need to complete (at a minimum) each day to help achieve your overall sales objectives. As discussed earlier in this book, success is measured in numbers and those numbers must "add up" on a daily basis in order to support your overall goals. Because of this, your keystone activities are those that must be completed every day, which ultimately lead to the greater goals you are trying to achieve on a weekly, monthly, quarterly, and annual basis.

For most salespeople, your daily activity checklist commonly will include certain keystone sales activities such as:

- ❑ Making at least (# here) cold phone calls each day
- ❑ Making at least (# here) follow-up phone calls each day
- ❑ Sending out at least (# here) prospecting emails each day
- ❑ Having at least (# here) new customer sales meeting
- ❑ Making at least (# here) new customer drop-ins

❏ Closing at least ($ here) in sales
❏ Closing at least (# here) new contracts

The goal with creating a daily activity checklist is to help you stay laser-focused on those activities that will help lead you to your sales objectives while de-prioritizing any distractions in the process. In essence, your daily activity checklist is your inflexible daily plan for success that holds you accountable by not allowing you to finish your workdays until all of your activities are completed. In order to create your own checklist, document the minimum level of activities you need to complete on a DAILY basis and modify as needed based on your results.

**Daily To-Do List.** Most salespeople today are bombarded with information and requests during the course of the workday that can easily distract them from completing their most critical daily sales activities first. The trick to playing good offense in sales is to prioritize your work and deal with those non-sales-related activities after your sales activities are completed. The best way to do this is to document them on a daily to-do list for later action—thereby delaying action without overloading your brain in trying to remember everything you still need to do.

Since you need to prioritize against daily distractions that come up during the course of the day that can take away from your goals, start each day by folding an 8 x 11 sheet of paper twice to write down the to-do items (non-goals-based activities) for completion later in the day. The benefit of the folded paper is also portability; it can be carried conveniently in your pocket without having to worry about battery life and multitasking on a single device.

Another option is to simply use the "notes" app on your smart phone, which, if you are like most people, is with you nearly all the time and anywhere you go. More advanced note-taking apps such as Evernote exist as well, so the more complex and collaborative your note-taking becomes, the more important using more advanced note-taking apps can become for you.

The bottom line is to first execute on your daily sales activity checklist—which you are accountable for in order to be successful—and not focus on distractions that can be completed later.

**Daily Calendar (Activity Schedules).** The final part of your planning and scheduling arsenal is your daily calendar, which details the chronology of ALL your daily activities, both personal and professional, for ALL 24 hours of your day. Below are a few examples used by successful salespeople today, and show how they are able to focus and effectively manage every minute of their day. Once you create your own calendar, make sure to document it in your current calendar management system and make sure that each task is recurring for each workday of the week—and hold yourself accountable to it.

Another benefit of using automation to calendar your days in advance is the ability to more strategically manage your time and any potential distractions with others. Now that they can see when you are able to work into their days, proper time expectations can be better met. Additionally, if you plan to buy time from other people to help support you and make you more productive, sharing and proper management of your calendar and time will become increasingly important.

By the way, daily calendars are nothing new. A man named Benjamin Franklin created his own "Daily Routine" hundreds of years ago—long before automation made this process much easier for you today. If he could do it then, you can certainly do it now!

| Time | Day Plan 1 | Day Plan 2 | Day Plan 3 |
|------|-----------|-----------|-----------|
| 5 am | Wake up | Wake up | Wake up |
| 5:10 am | Exercise | Exercise | Exercise |
| 6 am | Eat breakfast with family | Shower and get ready for work | Eat breakfast and read |
| 6:30 am | Shower and get ready for work | Commute | Shower and get ready for work |
| 7 am | Commute to work | Breakfast sales meeting | Commute to work |
| 7:30 am | Arrive at work | | Arrive at work |
| 8 am | | Arrive at work | |
| 10 am | Check emails and messages | Check emails and messages | Check emails and messages |
| 10:30 am | Work | Work | Work |
| 12 noon | Lunch sales meeting | Lunch sales meeting | Lunch sales meeting |
| 1 pm | Check emails and messages | Check emails and messages | Check emails and messages |
| 1:30 pm | Work | Work | Work |
| 4 pm | | | Check emails and messages |
| 4:30 pm | | | Commute home |
| 5 pm | Check emails and messages | Check emails and messages | |
| 5:30 pm | Work | Work | |
| 6 pm | Commute home | Commute home | Dinner sales meeting |
| 6:30 pm | Dinner (with family) | Dinner (with family) | |
| 7 pm | Family/personal time | Family/personal time | Family/personal time |
| 9 pm | Go to bed | Go to bed | Go to bed |

**EXAMPLE: DAILY ACTIVITY SCHEDULES**

# Benjamin Franklin's Daily Routine
## Source: Autobiography

| | | |
|---|---|---|
| The morning question, What good shall I do this day? | 5 | Rise, wash, and address *Powerful Goodness;* contrive day's business and take the resolution of the day; prosecute the present study; and breakfast. |
| | 6 | |
| | 7 | |
| | 8 | |
| | 9 | Work. |
| | 10 | |
| | 11 | |
| | 12 | Read or overlook my accounts, and dine. |
| | 1 | |
| | 2 | |
| | 3 | Work. |
| | 4 | |
| | 5 | |
| | 6 | Put things in their places, supper, music, or diversion, or conversation; examination of the day. |
| | 7 | |
| | 8 | |
| | 9 | |
| Evening question, What good have I done today? | 10 | |
| | 11 | |
| | 12 | |
| | 1 | Sleep. |
| | 2 | |
| | 3 | |
| | 4 | |

# CHAPTER 7

# EXERCISE THE MIND

• • •

*"If I have nine hours to chop down a tree,
I'd spend the first six sharpening my axe."*
*— Abraham Lincoln*

Growing up, I never lived what many people would consider to be a "normal" childhood. There never seemed to be enough sporting seasons to keep me at a point where I was able to learn at a pace that kept me fully engaged. Some sports seemed easier than others, and it was typically the most complex and unconventional "others" that grabbed my full attention. This is what led me to NASCAR in my early teens.

Most fifteen-year-olds dream of one day getting their driver's license, while I endeavored to build my first race car before I even had a driver's license. I was constantly asked by others how I knew how to build high-performance engines and cutting-edge race cars. The fact is I didn't. Instead, I had to learn—and fast! But what allowed me to learn how to do it were all of the books, publications, and questions I asked of others who did know. As a result, I quickly learned at a very early age that all of the knowledge I needed to accomplish nearly anything I wanted in life was already out there; most of which is published and freely available. Absent the ability to read, **there is no excuse why anybody cannot learn nearly anything they need to based on the published learnings of others.**

Years later, during my business career, I learned that I was not alone in my obsessive desire to read and learn, for it was shared by other people I also admired. In a 2007 commencement speech given at the USC Gould School of Law, Charlie Munger, one of the world's wealthiest businessmen and partner with Warren Buffett at Berkshire Hathaway, said, "I constantly see people rise in life who are not the smartest, sometimes not even the most diligent, **but they are learning machines. They go to bed every night a little wiser than they were when they got** up, and boy, does that help, particularly when you have a long run ahead of you."

Warren Buffett shared in his partner's sentiments. When asked by a student how to get smarter, Warren once held up a stack of papers and replied: **"Read 500 pages like this every day. That's how knowledge works. It builds up, like compound interest. All of you can do it, but I guarantee not many of you will."**[1]

## WHY WE LOVE TO LEARN

Think about what it feels like to learn something new. Or how about when you read a book that you can't seem to put down? How did that make you feel when you were done? Most people may love to read because it entertains and provides them with knowledge, but it does far more than that—and it all starts in the human brain.

Humans are genetically wired to explore and learn—that is why we are able to fly to the moon while most animals still only care about their own daily survival. The human brain also rewards us for learning, which in turn helps it to literally rewire itself and grow. When the human brain learns, neurons in the brain begin firing with other neurons (through new synapses), resulting in your brain actually getting bigger in size and you growing more intelligent in the process. So much for those who claim to get nothing from learning in school!

To help encourage this learning process, the human brain will release the neurotransmitters dopamine and serotonin along with hormones called BDNF when you learn. These rewards help provide you with feelings of happiness and an elevated mood after you learn. For this reason alone, **reading and exercise are commonly considered**

**to be some of the best ways to help prevent depression** since each are rewarded by the human brain when acted upon.

So the next time you need to find ways to help fight depression and find more happiness in your life, pick up an educational book and learn. Your brain will thank you for it, and so will your career.

## THE COMPOUNDING INTEREST OF KNOWLEDGE

Intelligent investors will commonly talk about the compounding interest of money and the power it provides. When money is compounding, it is building up more money based on the return (interest) received from an increasingly larger amount of money reinvested from the growing returns. Over time, this compounding (or growing) of money results in higher financial rewards. This is why investors will tell you that the earlier in life you start saving, the greater the potential reward when you decide to retire. Learning is no different.

The human brain has an incredible capacity to learn and store information, but it is not infinite. If it was, we wouldn't need to document what we learn. The human brain, especially when we sleep, will cull unused information connections (synapses), making room for new information and helping to strengthen what we commonly need to repeatedly know and get better at. In short, the human brain will "clean house" every night to make room for newer and better things. Because of this, what you do and how you think are signals to the brain as to what you want to keep in your house and make improvements to and what you don't.

Beyond these systemic limitations, the brain still has an enormous capacity to learn and wants to learn more and newer information each day. The good news is that the information you gain will build up (or compound) the more you read and learn, making you increasingly more knowledgeable and potentially valuable in your career.

Even though your mind will commonly "disconnect" the unused portions of what you have learned in the past, continuing to use what you do retain can only make you more intelligent. If you decide to one day use something you had learned in the past, you are telling your brain that it is now of value and needs to be cultivated again. That is why some things may look familiar to you but you may need more information/association to help remember them in more detail again.

## USING KNOWLEDGE AS A COMPETITIVE ADVANTAGE

Mark Cuban has quickly become a household name to many people in the sports and business communities, and for good reason—nearly everything he touches seems to turn to gold. Whether it be his flamboyant ownership of the Dallas Mavericks or his role on the hit TV series *Shark Tank,* Cuban seems to succeed at everything he tries. Cuban is also an avid reader—putting in at least three hours a day of pure reading.[2]

In his book *How to Win at the Sport of Business,* Cuban fondly stated the importance of reading in his career when he said, "I read every book and magazine I could . . . Most people won't put in the time to get a knowledge advantage. Sure, there were folks that worked hard at picking up every bit of information that they could, but we were few and far between. To this day, I feel like if I put in enough time consuming all the information available, particularly with the Internet making it so readily accessible, I can get an advantage in any technology business."

Clearly, business leaders like Warren Buffett, Mark Cuban, and the like were not born with the knowledge to accomplish what they did. Rather, they had to learn it, and they used that ability to learn more than their competition to their own advantage. In the business world today, there are literally thousands of books containing thousands of lifetimes' of learning and information, and all of them are within your own reach!

Despite the fact that nearly all of the information is now available to nearly everybody, it will never become a competitive advantage for you until you decide how to find it, when to consume it, and how to use it to your advantage. As Warren Buffett indicated, most people will not consume as much information as he will—despite his recommendation to do so. It is that action that becomes one of his greatest competitive advantages, and it should become yours as well.

## LEARN FROM YOUR CUSTOMERS
## AND SALES PROSPECTS

One of the greatest advantages you have as a salesperson is your direct and immediate access to customers and sales prospects. The insights you can receive through these unique interactions—by observing and asking a lot of questions—can allow you to learn more about your business and become more of an "expert" in your career. As a result, you need to start looking at your sales interactions as accomplishing two goals: getting the sale and learning from your customers for the next sale. You can lose one and learn but if you lose both you have failed.

By understanding that every interaction is both a chance to sell and a chance to learn, you should never again walk away from a customer sales engagement feeling like you gained nothing if you lost the sale. Some of my greatest lessons came from loses, and so will yours—but only if you learn from them. Remember: The difference between success and failure is what you learned through the process. Choose not to learn and you will fail—plain and simple. And one of the greatest opportunities you have to learn will come from your customers and prospects.

So the next time you lose a sale, ask yourself this simple question: What did I learn from this sale and will it make me a better salesperson in the future?

## CREATE DAILY LEARNING HABITS—STARTING TODAY!

I have established a personal goal to read at least two books a month, and spend a total of two hours a day for all of my reading. I do not read fiction, and my goals in reading each book and source are to learn and grow. I have countless boxes of books in my garage to attest to this goal. I believe that it is just as important to exercise the mind as we do the body, and reading is the best way to exercise my mind on a constant basis.

If you want to become successful in sales, you need to know that learning should never stop. The minute you stop learning is the minute you stop innovating. If you are not innovating, you are not growing—in business and in life. If you want to become successful, you need to **learn how to become successful.** And that is exactly what millionaires do.

Studies show that fully **88 percent of self-made millionaires will read at least 30 minutes each day**—and many will read far more than that. Warren Buffett has frequently stated over the years that he will typically spend upwards of 80 percent of his day reading. Most millionaires' reading is "educational" reading, with the goal of acquiring and maintaining knowledge. Interestingly, a large number of millionaires will also read biographies of other successful people, self-help and personal improvement books, and history books, as well as listen to audio books and podcasts while driving.

This same study also reveals a stark contrast in reading between millionaires and poor people. Ninety-two percent of poor people studied indicated that they DO NOT read to learn, and 79 percent of those who did read will only read for entertainment purposes.[3] The bottom line is if success requires knowledge and growth, you need to read to learn and improve.

If your goal is to become a millionaire salesperson, start by scheduling at least 30 minutes each day for educational reading—no exceptions! You will also be in good company since 82 percent of recently studied top-performing salespeople indicate that they strive for higher levels of knowledge and information.[4] Once you start your daily reading habit, don't be surprised when your time reading increases along with your sales knowledge and results. Here are some of the books I highly recommend to other salespeople to start with. Order them online now and get started today . . . no more excuses!

## SALES BOOKS

- *Influence: The Psychology of Persuasion.* Robert B. Cialdini, 2007
- *Sell Yourself First: The Most Critical Element in Every Sales Effort.* Thomas A. Freese, 2010
- *How to Sell Anything to Anybody.* Joe Girard with Stanley H. Brown, 2005

- *The Challenger Sale: Taking Control of the Customer Conversation.* Matthew Dixon and Brent Adamson, 2011

- *How to Win Customers and Keep Them for Life.* Michael LeBoeuf, Ph.D., 1987

- *Real Leaders Don't Do Power Point: How to Sell Yourself and Your Ideas.* Christopher Witt with Dale Fetherling, 2009

- *What Great Salespeople Do: The Science of Selling Through Emotional Connection and the Power of Story.* Michael Bosworth and Ben Zoldan, 2012

- *The Top 20%: Why 80% of Small Businesses Fail at Sales and Marketing and How You Can Succeed.* Dustin W. Ruge, 2015

- *Winning with Integrity: Getting What You're Worth Without Selling Your Soul.* Leigh Steinberg and Michael D'Orso, 1998

## COMMUNICATIONS / PRODUCTIVITY BOOKS

- *How to Win Friends & Influence People: The Only Book You Need to Lead You to Success.* Dale Carnegie, 1981

- *The Power of Habit: Why We Do What We Do in Life and Business.* Charles Duhigg, 2012

- *The Millionaire Next Door: The Surprising Secrets of America's Wealthy.* Thomas J. Stanley and William D. Danko, 1996

- *Outliers: The Story of Success.* Malcolm Gladwell, 2008

- *Change Your Habits, Change Your Life: Strategies That Transformed 177 Average People into Self-Made Millionaires.* Tom Corley, 2016

- *The 4-Hour Workweek: Escape 9–5, Live Anywhere, and Join the New Rich.* Timothy Ferriss, 2007

## HIRING BOOKS

- *Never Hire a Bad Salesperson Again: Selecting Candidates Who Are Absolutely Driven to Succeed.* Dr. Christopher Croner and Richard Abraham, 2006

- *Ultimate Guide to Platform Building.* Wendy Keller, 2016
- *The Successful Sales Manager: A Sales Manager's Handbook for Building Great Sales Performance.* Dustin W. Ruge, 2014

## BUSINESS BOOKS

- *The E-Myth Revisited: Why Most Small Businesses Don't Work and What to Do About It.* Michael E. Gerber, 1995

- *The Innovator's Dilemma: When New Technologies Cause Great Firms to Fail.* Clayton M. Christensen, 2000

- *The Goal: A Process of Ongoing Improvement.* Eliyahu M. Goldratt, 2004

- *The Loyalty Effect: The Hidden Force Behind Growth, Profits, and Lasting Value.* Frederick F. Reichheld and Thomas Teal, 1996

- *The Google Story: Inside the Hottest Business, Media, and Technology Success of Our Time.* David A. Vise and Mark Malseed, 2005, 2008

- *NUTS!: Southwest Airlines' Crazy Recipe for Business and Personal Success.* Kevin and Jackie Freiberg, 1996

- *Uncomplicate Business: All It Takes Is People, Time, and Money.* Howard Farran, 2015

- *Grinding It Out: The Making of McDonald's.* Ray Kroc with Robert Anderson, 1977

- *Sam Walton: Made in America.* Sam Walton with John Huey, 1992

- *Leadership Secrets of Attila the Hun.* Wess Roberts, Ph.D., 1985

# CHAPTER 8

# BUILD ENERGY, ATTITUDE, AND PASSION

• • •

*"The only way to do great work is to love what you do."*
— *Steve Jobs*

Do you start your workdays feeling like you're "tap dancing to work"? Warren Buffett does. Warren Buffett, commonly referred to as the "Oracle of Omaha," is now one of the most admired and richest men in the world. When people ask Warren what his secret to success is, his common reply is "find your passion."

In a 2012 interview with *Fortune,* Buffett had the following career advice: "Find your passion. I was very, very lucky to find it when I was seven or eight years old . . . You're lucky in life when you find it. And you can't guarantee you'll find it in your first job out. But I always tell college students that come out [to Berkshire Hathaway's annual meetings in Omaha], **'Take the job you would take if you were independently wealthy. You're going to do well at it.'"**[1]

Warren first found his passion for selling and investing by selling Cola-Cola to his friends, family, and neighbors at the age of seven. At the time, Buffett would buy a six-pack for a quarter and then sell them individually for a nickel. After years of sales, profits, and savings, he was able to buy his first stock at the age of eleven. Today, Warren Buffett's company, Berkshire Hathaway, Inc., is now the single largest shareholder of The Coca-Cola Company. Clearly Warren's passion for Coca-Cola has never waned—nor has his passion for selling and investing.[2]

If you talk to most self-made millionaires, you will find a common theme among them: They all had a dream and they passionately pursued that dream. Many people refer to living their dream as finding "their calling" in life—something that unfortunately seems to elude most people today. The starting point for finding your passion starts with discovering your primary purpose in life—which we discussed in chapter 2 of this book.

Your primary purpose is where your dreams receive focus and meaning and can then ultimately become your reality. Just like Warren's dream was to become an investor, Linda's dream was to provide her children with a better life. You have a primary purpose as well—whether you are aware of it or not.

The bottom line is if you want to really find your highest levels of success in your own life, you must have passion in order to achieve it. Passion is what motivates ordinary people to produce extraordinary results in life. **Passion creates a sense of obsession, determination, persistence, energy, and focus to the point that there never seems to be enough time left in your day and your work doesn't feels like "work" any longer.** When people reach this point in their career and life, that is when they typically find the greatest levels of happiness and wealth as a result. If this describes you, then you have found your passion. If it doesn't, then you need to keep looking for it.

But when you find it, don't confuse money for passion. This has led many people to trade money for their passion, thinking that the money in and of itself would create the passion—and they were wrong. You will commonly see this when you hear people say things like, "I hate this job but it pays well." Recent studies of salespeople have shown that **78 percent of salespeople say they would accept lower compensation to sell a product or service that is more compelling.**[3] If you truly set out to find and follow your passion, one (passion) may simply lead to another (money). Moreover, many people start out following their passion only to be rewarded later in money for that passion.

Just look at Southwest Airlines and their passion for customer service. Anybody who has ever flown Southwest knows about the colorful flight attendants and the unusually high levels of customer service provided compared to other major carriers. Southwest Airlines was founded in 1967, and in 1971 began to provide nonstop service to three airports in Texas with only three planes. At the time, these direct flights went against the major carriers' "hub and spoke" system of flight connections, but since then has helped Southwest Airlines become one of the largest and most respected airlines in the United States. Herb Kelleher, co-founder of Southwest Airlines, once said, "We tell our people, 'Don't worry about profit. Think about customer service.' Profit is a by-product of customer service. It's not an end in and of itself." Clearly the results speak for themselves.[4]

## ATTITUDE: MAKE IT CONTAGIOUS

Have you seen the 2015 Coca-Cola commercial with the guy laughing out loud and then getting the other riders on the New York City subway to do the same?[5] Brilliant! I have been on those very same subways for years and I can fully relate to this experience . . . New York subways could use more smiles and laughter.

But what makes this ad so special is what it teaches us about attitude—namely that **attitude and emotion are contagious!** Attitude is the one thing we all have 100 percent control of each day—yet we too often give up that control to others at our own expense. Did you know that the average two-year-old laughs 300 times a day while the average forty-year-old laughs only three times?[6] Amazing how just growing up affects our attitudes . . . so don't let it happen to you! Perhaps this would help explain why so many people love their dogs as well. After all, the average dog has been found to have the same intelligence level as a two-year-old child.[7] Coincidence?

One of the role models in my life when growing up was my Grandmother Hazel. Growing up with Hazel was a life lesson in attitude and how important it truly is—she had a magnetic attitude that drew people to her. Nobody wants to be around people with a bad attitude— it's poisonous and infectious and can ruin the day of anybody around them. **Negative people make positive people mentally sick when they**

**are around them.** People have a tendency to stay away from people with bad attitudes as well. Think about it: How many times have you asked to have dinner with somebody who always seems miserable? This is the same subconscious decision process that occurs when it comes to doing business with other people. And if you are in sales, it can be a killer.

In my last book, *The Top 20%: Why 80% of Small Businesses Fail at Sales and Marketing and How You Can Succeed,* I talk about a recent study regarding smiling and how we view "happy" people with a higher level of honesty, reliability, and TRUST. And TRUST is the one thing everybody wants to generate with others in today's business world—especially in sales. The growing majority of sales today involve services, and when you sell services, you are really selling a relationship and a promise of results—all predicated on the perceived level of trust you provide to the sales prospect.

As a result, I always tell others that **attitude starts with the seller, not the buyer.** Prior to any sale, the buyer will not commonly change the attitude of the seller, but the seller can change the attitude of the buyer. So the more you take control of your attitude each day, the better your results will be.

We also better know how the human brain works now. For example, what happens when somebody yawns around you? Most people will yawn in response. Why? Were you tired? Did you plan on yawning right after them? Most people cannot explain why this happens, but thanks to recent discoveries by neuroscientists, we now have a much better idea. The human brain is made up of tens of billions of cells called "neurons" that send chemical signals to other neurons—some of which have mirroring behaviors. These "mirror neurons" basically respond to (or mirror) the actions we observe in others—hence your yawning when others yawn.[8]

Many scientists now believe that because mirror neurons are developed prior to the age of one in humans, one of their main functions is to allow infants to better understand and mirror adult behaviors—which has historically led to better survival instincts at a very early age. Clearly these neurons stick with us throughout our lives and help explain what many people have always chalked up to the simple concept of "monkey see, monkey do."

So how can you use this mirroring of human behavior to your advantage? Here are a few tips to help you mirror the best reactions from your customers:

- **Don't meet with new clients and prospects while you are in a bad mood.** Bad moods internally will often be reflected in how you act externally, and it will show—especially on your face and in the reactions from your customers. If you're having a really bad day and you have important sales meetings, simply reschedule them for a time when your bad mood goes away.

- **Train yourself to smile more around other people.** If actors can train themselves to do this on stage, you can train yourself to do this in real life. Always start your greetings with a smile, eye contact, and a firm handshake. Make everybody you meet with feel like they are the most important person to you at that time.

- **Surround yourself with positive people who can help lift you up.** If you are in a bad mood, simply tell them in advance so they can help cheer you up or understand why you may need personal recovery time—whatever it takes to help change your mood. Every successful person I know has a swim buddy to help them get through the tough times (just like the Navy SEALs do). Just as you want to surround yourself with positive people, you need to avoid negative people as well. You can start by turning off the TV—there are no more miserable and negative people in the world today than in the major media.

- **Work for companies that hire for attitude.** Companies like Southwest Airlines have a motto to "hire for attitude, train for skill."[9] Ideally these are the types of companies you want to work for because skills can always be taught and changed but the attitudes of the people they hire typically cannot. Because of this, it is much more effective to "hire right" if you want to work in a culture of positive, like-minded people. One of the most effective ways I've found to help identify these types of people is to ask others who have previously worked with a job candidate two simple questions: **"What is it like working with [candidates name]?"** and **"What could he/she personally improve on?"**

- **Count your blessings.** Most people will recover from a bad mood, so you might as well start now by remembering all the things you should be truly thankful for in your life. Watch or read an inspirational story, pick up a book and feed your mind, watch a great comedy—anything to help change your focus away from negative thoughts.

No matter how hard we try, we all still have bad days and, being human, we all have to fight away some degree of depression in our daily lives. Knowing this, one of the best ways to help ensure a positive attitude is through regular exercise.

## EXERCISE AT LEAST 30 MINUTES EACH DAY

With the body goes the mind. That was the lesson I learned early in life when I watched a man I loved like a father rapidly deteriorate before my eyes. My grandfather grew up in rural Kansas during the Great Depression and worked hard for everything he had in life. He was a devoted family man and was frequently the life of the party when he arrived at family functions. I was very young when my father passed away and my grandfather, in true form, took upon himself many of the fatherly roles that passed away with my father. He was truly a greater angel of our nature.

In the later years of my grandfather's life, he was told by his doctor that he would need a hip replacement, which would involve a lengthy recovery. This was clearly not something he wanted to pursue at that time in his life—especially after recovering from a quadruple bypass only five years before. As a result, his daily routine of high activity and walking on the treadmill stopped, and the rapid decline in his health both physically and mentally followed. It was an early life lesson I will never forget.

The importance of staying physically fit dates back thousands of years but has never again quite rivaled the focus it once received in ancient Greece. The Greeks believed that the development of the human body was equal in importance to the development of the human mind. It was their belief that the well-being of the human body preceded the well-being of the mind. This was clearly a lesson I learned from my own experiences with my grandfather long before I would later learn of it in my own readings.

The ancient Greeks are not the only people who knew the importance of daily exercise. Recent studies have also shown that **76 percent of self-made millionaires exercise at least 30 minutes or more each day.**[10] By exercise we are talking about any type of cardio activity, such as running, biking, using treadmills or elliptical machines, swimming, etc., that raises the heart rate for at least 20 minutes.

Many successful people also choose to exercise early in the morning before work. By joining the 5 a.m. Club, these people are able to find the personal time needed to exercise without distractions. They also love the added benefit of early exercise because it helps trigger the release of endorphins (energy) and dopamine and serotonin (positive moods), leading to higher levels of energy and a positive outlook throughout the workday ahead.

As if all this were not reason enough to regularly exercise, another added benefit of exercise is that it leads to higher brain function through the increased growth of neurons (brain cells), hormones called BDNF (brain connections), glucose (brain fuel), and increased levels of oxygen delivered to the brain. In short, the more regularly you exercise, the more your brain grows, the smarter you can become, the less depressed and more energetic you can feel, and the better you will look and feel about yourself. Now you can see why the ancient Greeks and many successful millionaires of today see the need for regular exercise.

# LOVE WHY YOU SELL AND DON'T SETTLE

*"If you love what you do you will never work another day in your life."*
*—Warren Buffett*

People like Warren Buffett are lucky because they love what they do and advise the world to do the same. As salespeople, there are a number of things we may sell that we know can provide value, or even that we truly believe in, but to say we "love" them would be a misuse of the true definition of the word. It's easy to understand the value of a screw or a manhole cover, but does that mean that we have to love them in order to love selling them?

**In the United States today, roughly one out of every nine people are selling something.** This means that there are nearly fifteen million people whose profession is to "sell" according to the US Bureau of Labor Statistics. Consider also that the average tenure of a salesperson today is around two years—meaning that over a potential sales career lasting at least 30 years, a salesperson will likely sell for upwards of 15 different companies, all of which will likely have their own products and services. Moreover, with the rapid pace of technology innovation, it is a safe bet that many of these products and services you will one day be selling haven't even been developed yet.[11]

**In the world of sales, most people don't actually love what they sell, but why they sell it.** We all want to passionately love what we sell in our lives, but most of us will rarely, if ever, get that opportunity. So the question of whether you love what you sell is simply the wrong question and will fail you over and over again over the course of your sales career. Rather, the real question you should be asking yourself is: Do you love selling?

When you talk to top-performing salespeople, they will commonly tell you why they got into sales and what they love about selling. Many will tell you that they love working with people, being competitive, solving problems and helping customers, not being stuck in an office, being in control of their income, etc. The list can go on and on. But as we discussed in chapter 4, success always has a number and if you want to become an expert in your selling career, you need to dedicate yourself to the years it will take to help you get there—no matter what you're selling.

But that dedication starts internally with really wanting to enjoy and become successful at sales. This will ultimately help you love what you do instead of clouding your career path by trying to always love what you sell—for this love of product and service will always fail you. In the real world today, companies, products, services, performance, etc., change all the time. What you may love to sell today you may despise tomorrow and vice versa. As a result, you need to accept this reality and try to treat sales like any other profession and always work to master it and make improvements.

Here are a few ways you can start to really love selling and make the most of your sales career:

- **Always sell to your customers' "why" instead of focusing on the "what."** The best salespeople will position a sale based on the benefit (or problem solved) that the product or services provides to each individual customer. This focus will allow you to clearly understand the true benefits of what you sell, and creating customer success stories is what will drive you to love selling more to others.

- **Always learn, improve, and get better.** In my career of selling for over two decades, I have been exposed to countless sales methodologies and best practices. And that was my choice—I wanted to learn them all and constantly get better at my profession. But when you get good at selling, you will quickly realize that you are always learning from your customers and with your customers, and becoming a master at problem-solving—which is the essence of learning. The day you stop learning and think you know everything there is to know about selling is the day you should retire.

- **Don't be afraid of change.** The one constant in sales, as in life, is change. The days of our parents and grandparents working for one company until they retire have mostly gone the path of the dinosaurs. If you want to become a millionaire salesperson, you must always fight the slothful urge of complacency and always be on the lookout for bigger and better things. One of the best ways to do this is to have a strong professional network always helping you move forward.

- **Celebrate your victories and learn from your losses.** There is no such thing as a "perfect sales job." Therefore, you will always win and lose sales in your career. The trick is to learn to expect it and know that with sales comes highs and lows. So make sure to celebrate your highs and learn from your lows—for if you always learn from a loss, you will never fail in your career growth.

- **Spend more time with your customers and less time in your office.** Studies have shown that top-performing salespeople spend 33 percent more time with customers than other sales-people.[12] Let's face it: If you are a good salesperson you like working with people and helping them solve their problems. Because of this, you need to remove internal distractions and open up more of your time for your customers. As a good friend and mentor once told me: **"Problems are in the office and solutions are in the field."**

   **Build and grow your own network of successful people.** Many of the best sales opportunities in your career will come to you if your network is large and strong enough to support them. Your goal, then, should be to never burn bridges with others and stay in touch with other successful people after a change. If there is a better career opportunity at a growing company elsewhere, don't be surprised when your network clues you in on it.

- **Leverage mentors and teachers.** Studies have shown that 93 percent of self-made millionaires had at least one career mentor in their lives and 68 percent claimed that their mentors were a "critical factor" in their success.[13] A good mentor will help you avoid mistakes and help point you in the right direction. Warren Buffett attributes a great deal of his success to his mentor Benjamin Graham, who wrote *The Intelligent Investor* in 1949. After reading Graham's book, Buffett later followed Graham to Columbia Business School, where he became his student. Buffett's mentor was such a powerful influence that Buffett's own roommate at the time, Truman Wood, described Buffett's obsession with Graham as "it was almost like he found a god."[14]

## DEVELOP GOOD SLEEP HABITS

Ironically, one of the best ways to improve your sales performance during your workdays has a great deal to do with how you sleep when you are not working. Many people today get "busy" in their lives and feel like they can cut corners on sleeping since it seems to be an unproductive use of time. But clearly they are wrong.

It is well known that Benjamin Franklin scheduled his sleep time, and so should you—for **no less than seven to eight hours each day.** Fully 89 percent of self-made millionaires get seven or more hours of sleep a night because they know that proper sleep is critical for success. Sleep loss ultimately results in mind loss, and in the simplest terms: It makes you stupid.[15]

We have all experienced what it feels like after a night of little or no sleep. The US Centers for Disease Control and Prevention estimates that **nearly one-third of all Americans are sleep deprived**—meaning they are receiving less than six hours of sleep a day.[16] People who do not get enough sleep tend to suffer from sub-standard thinking, loss of attention, memory loss, bad moods, poor logical reasoning, poor quantitative reasoning, and much more.[17] Neuroscientists have discovered that sleep is critical for a number of brain functions, including memory formation. Sleep essentially allows your brain time to process and remember what you learned the previous day. Therefore, depriving it of this critical time results in long-term memory storage problems.

Recent research has also found that sleep-deprived people have a difficult time reading facial expressions in other people—meaning they are less effective at reading body language, which can be critical in sales. Add to this a tendency to overreact to little things as well as higher levels of irritation, stress, anger, and anxiety, and all of a sudden losing sleep can cost you far more than simply losing sleep.[18]

Compare this problem to the times when you've woken up after a good night's sleep and are able to think clearly and quickly. This is the result of your brain being able to clean itself out while you sleep and make more room for it to able to learn and organize new information. [19] For example, think about the last time you started a new job. Job changes typically require a significant amount of new information to be processed in a short amount of time. The human brain will make room for this information by culling out neural (synaptic) connectors that are no longer in use to make room for new ones. In short, the memories (and thoughts) that you actively use the most are fed while those you don't get disconnected. This is why old information and habits are often easy to forget. Your brain helps to make these decisions for you when you sleep. It also serves as a warning that you can become what you think—literally!

Neuroscientists have also discovered that sleep enables the conscious mind (the neocortex) to better communicate with the sub-conscious mind (limbic system and reptilian brain), which leads to what we commonly recognize as "intuition." Since the conscious mind will shut down during sleep, it is better able to process subconscious sensory data and make decision making more instinctive.

So how do we know that seven to eight hours of sleep is optimal? Tom Corley writes is his book *Change Your Habits, Change Your Life* that the way you sleep is actually more important than the time you need to sleep. When we sleep, we go through a series of "sleep cycles," composed of five stages. Each one of these stages takes around ninety minutes to complete, with humans needing to complete at least four to five (five being ideal) stages per day—hence the seven to eight hours of sleep needed to complete all of these cycles.

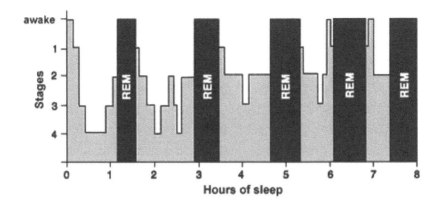

As we discussed in chapter 6, being on the offensive with your time and scheduling out all 24 hours of each day in advance is critical to proper time management and productivity. Part of that schedule should ALWAYS include at least seven to eight hours dedicated to sleep only. If you want to join the 5 a.m. Club, you will need to be in bed sleeping no later than 9 or 10 p.m. the night before. If you are living with your spouse and/or children, they should also clearly understand this sleep schedule so they do not interfere with it.

Changing your sleep habits is not difficult and is done successfully by others every day. Just look at US soldiers who first enter boot camp—one of their first habitual indoctrinations is to wake up at 5 a.m. sharp. At first, some soldiers struggle to develop this new habit, but many will tell you that **around week four, this becomes more natural and normal.** In other words, their brains have now been programmed to this new habit.

Of course, most people aren't wired to naturally wake up at 5 a.m. each day, so much like military personnel, you will need to train yourself to do it. In his book *The Power of When,* Dr. Michael Breus, commonly referred to as "the sleep doctor," has determined that most people have a genetic chronotype that typically comes from one of our parents. This chronotype, or your own biological ticking clock, determines your natural sleep patterns. Dr. Breus breaks these chronotypes into four categories.

The first category is referred to as "dolphin" and represents about 10 percent of the population. Dolphins are light sleepers and can be easily awakened. The second category is "wolf," which accounts for around 15–20 percent of the population. Wolves are typically "nighttime" people. The third category is "lion," which accounts for around 15–20 percent of the population. These are typically your early-morning people. The final category is "bear," which represents around 50 percent of the population. These people tend to time their sleep around sunrise and sunset. To find out which category you fall into, take the sleep quiz at www.thepowerofwhenquiz.com.

Based on numbers alone, the majority of people are "bears" by their natural disposition, which means they have to proactively modify their chronotype to join the 5 a.m. Club and be more like "lions"— which is where nearly half of all self-made millionaires now reside. The first goal in this journey is to make sure you get at least seven to eight hours of sleep a night. The second is to make sure you avoid weekly "jet lag" by maintaining the same sleep patterns every day of the week—not just during weekdays. The third goal is to better time your sleep for the highest levels of productivity.

As you can see, sleep is one of those critical keystone habits that can potentially impact (both negatively and positively) so many aspects of your day ahead. Because of this, it should receive the same level of importance as all of your other activities and be scheduled in the same manner.

# — CHAPTER 9 —

# COFFEE IS FOR CLOSERS

• • •

*"People don't ask for facts in making up their minds.
They would rather have one good,
soul-satisfying emotion than a dozen facts."*
— Robert Keith Leavitt

Who can forget the famous scene from the movie *Glengarry Glen Ross* when Alec Baldwin tries to motivate a group of salespeople by telling them to **"A"** Always, **"B"** Be, **"C"** Closing? The point was to make sure that no matter what happens in a sales process, they are always pushing to the same defined objective: the close. As entertaining and disturbing as this scene may be to some, it does help illustrate a part of the sales process where most people do in fact fail to execute effectively. If you are a successful salesperson, you are a closer. If you cannot or will not close a sale, you will never become a great salesperson.

As I do with all of the salespeople I work with, I sat Linda down and we started her training on closing first.

"Linda, how much closing training have you received in your sales career?" I asked.

Linda quickly and confidently responded, "I received sales training at my previous companies, and also when I started working here."

"Okay. And during all of those sales training sessions, how much of that time was specifically dedicated to closing tactics and best practices?" I asked.

"Well, they taught us how to create contracts and process orders once received," Linda replied with a rather confused look on her face.

"Is that what you're referring to?"

Most sales trainers will teach "selling" first and save closing for last—but I don't. If the salesperson cannot close, why waste valuable time and resources teaching them how to sell first? As in Linda's case, most companies don't even teach closing tactics at all to their salespeople yet will spend millions teaching them "how to sell" their products and services instead.

I turned my computer screen around so Linda could see it along with me. I opened up our sales (CRM) reporting tool and showed her two side-by-side reports with different results. I then asked her, "Have you ever seen this report?"

"Yes, we use that to track our sales pipeline and activity," replied Linda. "I see two reports, though, and the one on the left looks like my data."

"Correct. And do you know whose data is on the right?" I asked.

"No," replied Linda with an inquisitive look on her face while leaning in for a closer look.

"The report on the right is for Robert—the top salesperson for our company over the past three years," I replied. "And what do you see on his report that differs from yours?"

"Clearly he is selling a lot and making a lot of money here," Linda quickly replied.

"That's true, but I want you to look a little deeper as to why he's selling more than anybody else," I responded. "Take a look at the blue chart representing the number of total sales appointments. What do you notice about his chart compared to yours? "

Linda leaned in a little farther and with a puzzled look replied, "They are almost exactly the same."

"Right," I said. "Now look at the orange and green charts representing total orders received and average order value, and tell me what you see."

"Robert is getting a lot more orders and bigger sales than I am," replied Linda. "I always thought that Robert must have a lot more sales meetings than the rest of us, but I'm not seeing that here. There are a lot of people here like me who would be shocked to see those numbers."

"Exactly," I responded. "What these numbers tell you isn't that you aren't working hard enough or even that you're not getting enough sales meetings, but rather that you're not closing the same amount of selling opportunities and at the same price as Robert is. Think about this for a minute. You and Robert have the same amount of sales meetings, but if you could simply close as effectively as Robert does, you would be right there with him at the top."

Linda sat back in her chair and a smile came over her face. For the first time in Linda's sales career, she discovered what was truly holding her back. Linda's biggest problem was not that she wasn't selling enough but rather that she wasn't closing more of what she was already selling.

Most salespeople like Linda completely confuse selling for closing and tend to excel at the former and fail at the latter. But if the goal of selling is to get the sale, why do studies show that **78 percent of salespeople hesitate when it comes time to ask for the sale and 66 percent will end a sales meeting without asking at all?**[1] Worse yet, 44 percent of salespeople will give up on a sale after only one "no." So why do so many salespeople like Linda waste so much of their time and resources to prospect, generate leads, and conduct sales meetings and then never ask for the sale?

## WHY PEOPLE SAY "YES"

Getting people to close can be a very emotional experience for a salesperson—especially for someone like Linda who had not made it a habit to try to ask for the close during every sale. But just as it may be emotionally challenging for Linda, it is emotional for the buyer as well. So how are people like Linda selling to their potential buyers today? With little to no emotions and a whole bunch of facts. Square peg, round hole.

Recent studies have shown that **70 percent of people make purchasing decisions to solve a problem while only 30 percent do so to gain something.**[2] When people finally decide to buy, they buy based on only two factors: **greed or fear.** Most salespeople mistakenly sell to greed, forgetting that fear is the strongest emotion and is processed in the limbic system of the human brain. The limbic system also happens to be where the decision to say "yes" or "no" comes from first. So no matter how compelling your business's case to buy is, **the final decision compelling buyers to buy will be largely emotional.**

Fear can also work against you since it also leads buyers to a heightened state of risk avoidance. This was the premise behind the Prospect Theory (also referred to as the Loss Aversion Theory) first published in 1979, stating that the fear of loss causes a greater emotional impact on people than an equal level of gain. In short, people are more emotionally motivated to avoid a loss than to receive a gain.[3]

Because of this, you need to understand the psychological state of your buyer's mind at this critical time in the sales process and make sure that you are addressing and closing to their emotional needs and concerns instead of just the rational.

It is important to note here that for centuries most salespeople have been "trained" to sell based on facts and logic. But logic only resides in one part of our brain—and that part is not the limbic system, where the final emotional decision to say "yes" emanates from.

As previously discussed in this book, the human brain is made up of three major parts: the reptilian brain, which controls the body's vital "instinctive" functions such as your breathing, heart rate, balance, etc.; the limbic system (or limbic brain), which controls your motivations, emotions, learning, and memory; and the cerebral cortex, where more advanced and "higher-function" functions such as information processing, language, thinking, consciousness, etc., take place. The cerebral cortex generally divides functions between the right side of the brain, which involves creativity, and the left side the brain, which is more logically and analytically focused.

By strictly selling based on logic and facts, you are in effect selling to the left side of the buyer's brain. But when the final decision to buy is made, it comes from the buyer's limbic system, or the right side of the brain, and is then justified after the fact by the left side of the brain, using logic. In short, **emotion, not logic, is what drives a final decision to buy, and that is exactly what you should be selling to.** The higher the level of emotion, the more likely a decision to buy will be made.

For example, many of us know what it's like to purchase a new home. For most people, it is the largest purchasing decision they will make in their lives. When looking for homes, most buyers have logical criteria (greed) in mind for their new home, and when they find it, their emotional reaction will commonly be to buy it quickly due to their now-emotional connection to the property and the thought of potentially losing it (fear) if they don't act now. In these situations, the emotional connection and the potential fear of losing a property is the compelling event to buy now; the higher the emotional connection and levels of competition and/or the risk of loss, the greater the fear. Good real estate agents use this fear to their sales advantage.

Another example would be the future transition of a family farm upon the death of a parent. Most people don't want to think about the death of any family member, but it is the one common ending we all share—it's just a matter of how and when. Because of potentially high estate-inheritance taxes, many farmers could end up losing their family farm after death, when they would rather have it inherited by their children. An estate-planning attorney might explain how to set up trusts to help protect these family objectives, but how much more motivated would they likely be to act now if they knew that a parent's death could come any day? Moreover, how could that heightened emotional state be used to help trigger an action to set up a trust today as opposed to continuing to wait?

These examples exist in nearly all businesses and further illustrate the power that emotion truly has in closing business. Many salespeople fail to recognize this fact, and when a customer emotionally objects to a sell the salesperson will try to continue to close them based on logic and facts. That is the surest way to sell to the wrong source of the objection and need.

## PEOPLE BUY WHAT THEY WANT— NOT WHAT THEY NEED

Now that we know where and why buying decisions are made, it is equally important to dispel another myth in sales. Namely, that people buy what they "need." I cannot begin to tell you how many times I've heard salespeople try to sell to somebody's "needs" only to see them fail over and over again.

As we previously discussed, making a final buying decision is an emotionally based process. When somebody "needs" something, it is the logical part of their brain talking. But since most people don't make the final buying decision based on logic alone, there must be something else—and that something else is called "want." Because of this, most people do not buy based on needs (logic) but rather based on their wants (emotion).

To help illustrate this point, I recently worked with a client named Michael who had moved from being a very successful sales engineer to an outside sales rep within the same company. Michael was sent to me because he was consistently the top-performing sales engineer for many years and was considered to be a future leader of the company. The problem was that since Michael's recent transition into sales, his performance had dramatically tapered off and his managers were now concerned.

"How could this be?" asked one of his sales managers. "He knows our products and services better than any of my other sales reps. He should be a natural at this." I wish this was the first time I had heard this from another manager but unfortunately it was not.

When I first asked Michael to walk me through his sales and closing process, I noticed that he did a fantastic job at discovering my needs but he never really understood what I truly wanted. To Michael, it was only "logical" that, based on my needs alone, I should want to buy from him. As I discovered prior to our working together, this was a similar experience I'd observed with many of his sales prospects as well. So I stopped Michael during our process and asked him a simple question.

"Michael, what is it that I truly want?" I asked.

After a brief pause and a rather confused look Michael replied, "You said you needed— "

"Michael," I quickly said as I stopped him again mid-sentence. "I asked you what I wanted, not what I needed. Until you understand what I want, you are going to lose more sales until you get this right."

Michael sat back in his chair with a confused look on his face that reminded me of the look Spock would frequently display on *Star Trek* when something didn't sound "logical" to him. So I decided to provide my new Vulcan protégé with a little dose of human reality.

"Michael, let me ask you a question," I said. "Do you always buy what you need or do you buy what you want? For example, do you drive a car?"

"Of course," replied Michael. "How else do you think I got here today?"

"And what kind of car did you drive today to get here?" I asked.

"I own a Lexus GX400" Michael responded with a continued look of confusion.

"A Lexus GX400 is pretty nice car, Michael," I said. "Why did you need to buy such an expensive car in order to get here today? Certainly there are many other cars that could have gotten you here today at a fraction of the price, right?"

"I suppose," replied Michael. "But it's the best car I've ever owned and I love driving it."

"So what you're telling me is that you 'need' a car to get here but you 'want' to drive a Lexus GX400 because you said you love driving it," I said. "So when you bought your Lexus, did the car salesman sell you what you needed or what you wanted when you made your final decision to buy it?"

Most "logical" people like Michael commonly confuse "needs" with "wants" in nearly every part of their lives. For example, we all have a logical need to eat but what we choose to eat is typically what we want, not what is most needed by our bodies. We don't "need" a glass of wine, a large rib-eye steak, butter on our potatoes, and chocolate cake for dessert to satisfy our hunger—but we want it. We don't need to buy clothes at Nordstrom, Neiman Marcus, and Bergdorf Goodman, but many of us want to.

When is the last time you were in a health club? If you are like most people, you probably joined right after your New Year's resolution. And what did you notice when you first walked in? You probably saw a lot of "fit" people, which is likely what you and/or your significant other wants you to become by joining the club. The only problem is you most likely told yourself that you "need" to get fit while looking around at a whole bunch of people who are already fit. They are there because they "want" to stay fit while most other people, maybe even you, feel they "need" to be fit. Guess who will likely still be there in three months? It's the people who "want" to be there. Why? **Because "want" is an emotional need that through desire helps to will us on our way to that objective— the stronger the want, the stronger the will.**

Of course, I wasn't picking on Michael based on his choice of car, either. I have two cars in my garage and one of them is a Porsche 911 Carrera Cabriolet. Do I need to own a Porsche? Just ask my wife, who frequently reminds me that I "don't need that damn Porsche in the garage." And she's right—I don't. But I want it. I don't need it any more than she needs her 150 pairs of shoes in our closet.

The point is that we all do and buy things in our life that we "want" that based on "need" alone make no sense whatsoever. Most people need a lot of things—some of which they want to buy and some of which they don't. That is part of being human. And as a salesperson, you must know the difference or you'll end up right where Michael was.

"Michael, who are the people that need the products and services you sell today?" I asked.

"Any small business owner," replied Michael.

"Any small business owner?" I asked. "You mean any of the millions of small business owners in the US need your product?"

"That's what the company tells us, and our products really are better than our competitors in many ways," Michael replied confidently.

"So, Michael, does that mean that if any small business owner in the US meets with you, they will need your products and services?" I asked.

"They should," replied Michael. "Like I said, we're so much better than our competitors that it should be a no-brainer once I meet with them and discuss it."

"If you are so good at convincing them they need your products and services, then why is your close ratio one of the lowest on your sales team?" I asked.

"I don't know," said Michael. "They all seem to understand the need and the meetings seem to go great but then they go quiet on me and won't sign."

"They may all truly need your products and services, Michael, but until they want it, they will not buy it," I said.

**One of the first mistakes salespeople make is believing that the market for their products and services is much larger than it truly is.** Many companies perpetuate this belief in order to help motivate their salespeople and investors in believing that what's out there to sell is as close to infinite as possible. But the truth is far from it in most industries today.

This notion that "any business" is a potential customer is a myth and is the reason salespeople like Michael waste their time trying to sell to people who will not buy. As Michael had discovered the hard way, the need may truly exist with every potential buyer but the want to buy is frequently a much narrower market. Therefore, understanding what your true market is and what they want instead of just what they need is frequently the difference between success and failure in business.

Once Michael starts focusing on who these ideal customers are and what they really want both before he decides to meet with them and before he wastes any more of his limited time trying to close something that isn't closable, the less time he will waste, the higher his close ratio will climb, and the better salesperson he will become.

## THE FIVE WHYS OF CLOSING

There are five questions every buyer will ask themselves, consciously or not, when they decide buy. These are:

1. Why you?

2. Why your company?

3. Why change?

4. Why your product/service?

5. Why now?

The importance of these questions lies not only in the function of the questions but in the sequence of them as well. It is also important as the seller to be able to effectively address each of these questions and/or objections for each sale. Think of this questioning as sales steps in your sales process that each buyer must journey through to get to a close. Without addressing each step in this order, your sale is likely to not close.

For example, I remember one of the first new cars my wife wanted to buy. She knew which dealers she wanted to approach first (WHY THE COMPANY?), she knew why she needed a new car (WHY CHANGE?), she did her research and knew exactly what car she wanted to buy (WHY YOUR PRODUCT?), and she knew why she wanted to buy it that weekend (WHY NOW?).

See any missing steps in this process? Well, here is how it all started . . . and quickly ended. Upon arriving at the first car dealer, ready to buy, we encountered a car salesman who quickly approached us on the lot **(WHY YOU?).** Everything went downhill from there. How he treated my wife during our discussions and the test drive made it clear to my wife that she did not want to buy from him—despite being ready to move forward with the final four Whys. Even a quick attempt to save the deal by his manager as we stormed off the lot was unsuccessful, despite his offering a lower price than we ended up paying at another lot for the same car.

As you can see, although it was important for each step to be addressed in my wife's mind, getting past the first step is the most critical—and where most sales fail before they ever begin.

**WHY YOU?** ultimately comes down to two critical words: **CREDIBILITY** and **TRUST.** If you lack either of these qualities in the eyes of your buyer, you will fail to close business. In chapter 13 we will talk about the importance of becoming a unique, trusted advisor who people will want to work with. Gaining a heightened level of trust in the buyer's mind allows them to more easily and emotionally connect with you and want to make the emotional decision to say "yes." Let's face it: Salespeople have an inherent credibility gap in the minds of most people, so you have to take steps to help close that gap and make an emotional connection with the buyer.

Beyond trust, you must also command a high level of personal credibility in the buyer's mind. This means conveying a higher level of knowledge, expertise, and understanding of each customer's needs and wants and, most important, proving that what you provide has added value for similar customers. The best way to share these similar customer successes is through storytelling—as we will discuss in more detail in chapter 11.

The second question buyers will ask is **WHY YOUR COMPANY?** Now, if you and your company are one in the same, this is addressed in the WHY YOU? portion. But if you are selling for a company, once the buyer has accepted you they will need to accept your company as well. And for good reason: The average salesperson today will stay with a company for less than two years, while many products and services can remain in use with a buyer far longer than that.

WHY YOUR COMPANY? requires a level of credibility and trust with the company as well. If you are an established brand in the marketplace, it can be easier to establish credibility and trust with your buyers as long as your reputation supports it. If your company's reputation is lacking, most salespeople will compensate by building a stronger WHY YOU? message beforehand to help overcome it. In short, the weaker the company, the stronger the seller will need to be.

The third question, **WHY CHANGE?,** is perhaps the most important and where most salespeople fail. The easiest decision any buyer can make is to do nothing, and by not selling the buyer on the need to change, they will be inclined to do just that—nothing. The human brain is wired for safety and survival first, and therefore people have a natural fear of what they don't know and cling to what they do—even if what they know is not always the best option. There is an old saying: The devil you know is better than the devil you don't. Unless the change you are selling is clearly recognizable in the buyer's mind, your close rates will dramatically drop.

Many of the products and services sold today can be confusing to the average buyer, especially those that are technologically driven. Albert Einstein famously said, "If you cannot explain it simply, you don't understand it well enough." And if it can be confusing to you, it sure as hell will confuse your buyer. Bottom line: A confused mind will always say "no"—leading to no change.

**Most sales will end up in inaction, and many times this has to do with the confused mind of the buyer.** If your buyer is not clear on the value proposition you're providing to them, they will likely not give you a second chance to explain it—most people are busy enough. Instead, they'll commonly "go quiet" or simply tell you that the price was "too high" so they can get you to stop the sales process with them.

It's important to note here that the job of a salesperson is not to be smarter than their prospective customers. In reality, the job of a salesperson is to take their vast store of knowledge and translate it in a way that the prospective customer can clearly understand. This means not using special acronyms, jargon, or other forms of communication that the client does not understand. You have to be able to speak at their level first so they can understand your value exchange and, in doing so, also build up credibility and trust so they can better rely on your expertise to handle the more confusing aspects of your products and services. Remember, **people don't want another salesperson—they want a trusted advisor.**

The fourth question, **WHY YOUR PRODUCT/SERVICE?,** is ironically where most "sales training" within companies takes place today. The focus here is on positioning your products or services as a competitively superior value in the mind of the buyer.

In order to successfully sell your products or services, you need to create a heightened level of curiosity in the buyer's mind about your offerings. The traditional sales approach of leading with facts and functions will not help create curiosity because curiosity is a function of the limbic system of the brain, where emotions reside. Because of this, you need to connect emotionally with the buyers based on the "why" of your products and services first—not the "how" and "what."

A few years back, author Simon Sinek did an analysis of why some organizations succeed and why most fail over time. In doing so, he developed what he referred to as the Golden Circle.[4] This simple concept was based on the premise that **people don't buy what you do but rather why you do it.** His theory was based on the notion that in most organizations today, the vast majority of people know the "what" of their jobs, fewer know the "how" of their jobs, and very few, if any, truly know the "why" of their organizations. By losing focus of the "why," most organizations will end up valuing process over purpose, and thereby lose their direction and ultimately fail to grow and succeed.

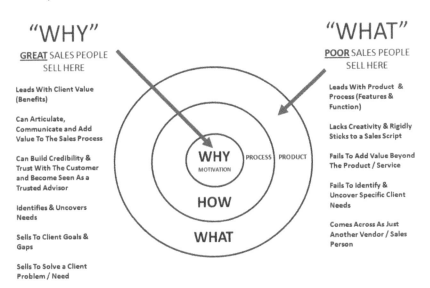

What makes the Golden Circle so powerful is that it equally applies to sales and marketing. As the amount of advertising and constant sales bombardment our prospects receive grows each year, people are becoming increasingly jaded to sales activities and less receptive to new sales solicitations. As our economy continues to mature, many of the products and services we sell are becoming increasingly commoditized, price sensitive, and more reliant on skilled sales and marketing than ever before. As a result, you need to become more focused on the value your products and services provide to each customer than the old-school notion of letting the products and services "sell themselves." We do this by learning how to better sell to the "why" of each customer.

When I work with salespeople I teach them to stop talking about product and service features and instead start articulating the value and benefits that those products and services provide to each prospective customer. The most effective way to do this is by training to **sell to each buyer's goals and gaps.** By understanding a customer's goals, you can determine the "why" of their potential motivations. The gaps are determined by simply understanding what they do now and what else is needed to get them to their goals (WHY CHANGE? and WHY OUR PRODUCTS/SERVICES?). Ideally these gaps will then open the door for whatever services you can provide.

Creating curiosity is also a time-sensitive practice—especially when dealing with new buyers. We know from studies that the average person will focus on your sale for no more than 10–20 seconds before deciding to either continue or send you off.[5] This means that you have a VERY short window to rapidly build enough curiosity to continue with the sale. Which takes us to our final "why."

The fifth and final question, **WHY NOW?,** is another area of frequent failure for salespeople. **The greatest closing tactic in any sale includes the creation of urgency through scarcity.** When it comes to selling, nothing sells better than scarcity because **people will demand more of what they can have less of.** What makes scarcity so powerful in sales is that it helps create a sense of urgency that leads to action—oftentimes when a business may need sales the most. This typically includes times when seasonality can lower sales volume, when resources and inventory are too high and need liquidation, or when you simply need more sales to hit your sales goals. No matter that your needs, scarcity can do what in many ways even price discounting cannot; namely, to get people to buy fast and buy now!

WHY NOW? is also predicated on the two things customers must know to create urgency and action in sales: the benefit of the action and the opportunity cost to them of inaction. Unlike most other closing tactics that are designed around the benefits to a customer, scarcity is the opposite due to its **focus on the cost of inaction.**

For example, in 2003 British Airways announced the end of their Concorde flights between London and New York due to costs. The result: Sales following the announcement increased dramatically for their remaining flights. Why? Did the service somehow improve over the last few flights? No. What changed was scarcity—people knew that this could be their last opportunity to experience a Concorde flight. The inherent value of the flight didn't increase after the announcement but rather the value to the customer based on scarcity of the unique flights remaining did.

Scarcity can be used in the sale of any product or service **as long as there is uniqueness to the offer.** If you plan to make something scarce when selling, it has little or no effect if your customers have alternative places to buy it. This is especially true in today's business environment where nearly anything can be found and ordered over the Internet. But don't worry if you sell similar products or services to others, for scarcity in uniqueness can be applied to anything, such as unique services, unique delivery and fulfillment options, unique timing, and unique incentives and pricing.

In the professional services industry one of the **most valuable resources is time.** And since it is limited, it can be used very effectively to your sales advantage. For example, if you are a service provider, when was the last time you contacted a prospective customer to let them know you had a rare opening in your schedule to potentially work them in next week and you were contacting them first? And if they didn't take it, somebody else would. What did you just do? You used scarcity of access by letting one or more prospects know that they could uniquely take advantage of this scarcity in the opening of your schedule for a limited time.

Another example would be a scarcity in pricing. When was the last time you were offered a discount on services from another professional, such as a discount on dental work, insurance, websites, tax preparation, etc.? Most people receive these, but they are still not compelling enough because they are not unique in service and/or typically don't **include a short deadline for action.** In fact, many discounted offers include no deadline at all, and even if they do, the time frame is often too long—sometimes a month or more. Why does this not work? Because without a shortened deadline, people will typically procrastinate and make the easiest decision of all by doing nothing. How do you combat this? By providing greater incentives with shorter deadlines.

Think about it: What do you do when you open and sort through your mail? You are quickly making a decision of action or inaction. If I have one piece of mail offering a 10 percent discount on services that I can use at any time versus another that offers a 25 percent discount for the same services but expires in five days, which one is more unique, compelling, and likely to get my attention and action? This brings us to the final part of using scarcity, which is the **expectation of uniqueness.** In this example, how many times will I see the 25 percent discount offered and how many times is too many times to where I then feel compelled to wait for the next expected offer to arrive in order to act—if I act at all? Moreover, if I receive these with such high frequency, will I never again utilize services from this service provider at full price, knowing that I can instead wait to act on these discounts alone? Just look at all the pizza coupons still sitting in your drawers to help illustrate this point.

The idea here is to make sure that whatever scarcity you create is not an expected scarcity that repeats with commonality. If people regularly expect an offer from you to compel them to buy, then you are now competing based largely on price—which, unless you plan to scale your business larger than your competitors, you cannot win at in the long term. So be careful and calculated with your scarcity offers so your customers are not expecting the scarcity you wish to create based on pricing. Here are a few ways to do this:

First, make sure any unique pricing offer you provide is **not repeated for at least 6–12 months.** In order to maintain a level of expected uniqueness in your pricing offers, you should not have too high a frequency, which can lead your customers to consistently expect to receive them in order to buy from you. If you do have a need to increase your frequency of unique offers, then change the parameters of the offer, such as the pricing discount relative to the deadline, with the higher discounts offered in the shortest time frame and vice versa. Remember, if your customers see the same offers too often and learn to expect them in order to act, you are becoming a business who now competes where nobody wants to: based on price. In short, don't become another pizza company in your marketing.

Second, make sure any pricing offer has a **VERY short deadline,** such as a week or less from the expected time of delivery. **Giving people too much time to decide is helping them make the easiest decision of all, which is to do nothing.** Since most purchasing decisions end in no decision, you are in effect helping your biggest competitor sell against you by giving deadlines that are too long or, worse yet, giving no deadlines at all. Good scarcity marketing and selling requires action, and without a compelling deadline, most customers will choose inaction instead.

Third, **DO NOT accept expired pricing promotions** when used. How many times have you initially offered a discount only to have a customer wait and then expect that same discount from you in the future? We all have. Be firm on your published deadlines, for they will set a precedent for the uniqueness of your offers and how people will react to future pricing promotions from you once received. Any exception to this rule sends a clear signal to your customers and prospects that your pricing offers are far less unique than you want them to be. Moreover, by not accepting them you are enforcing an opportunity cost of inaction, which is the basis for effective scarcity marketing.

Fourth, when possible, **offer better pricing promotions for shorter deadlines** and vice versa. If you want people to act now, give them a good reason to do it. If your service costs $500, how compelling would a 1 percent discount be as opposed to a 30 percent discount? In every business, you need to determine what that percentage or dollar value is that will tip the scales in your favor and compel customers to want to buy.

It's also important to make sure you communicate your own shorter deadlines when selling—even if your company may offer longer time frames. Remember, unless you, your company, or other customers tell them otherwise, how else would your sales prospects know what your real discounts are and when they expire? In most sales situations they don't—so stop acting like they somehow do and create your own deadlines and discounts based on what the company provides YOU to work with first.

# CHAPTER 10

# COMPARED TO WHAT?

• • •

*"People's buying decisions are governed by their own
unique perspectives. Therefore, unless you can fully
understand and help define that perspective when you sell,
you will be selling against another unknown
reality in the minds of your buyers."*
— Dustin Ruge

Linda had just walked into my office the morning after a sales call we'd gone on together. That sales call ended in a much smaller sale then she'd anticipated. I could tell she was getting frustrated—this was the sale she needed to get over quota for the month and it came in at a fraction of the price she wanted. We'd now been on over a dozen sales meetings together and although she was making progress, her average order values and closing rates were still low.

"Linda, how did you think the sales meeting went yesterday?" I asked while sitting at my desk.

"Not so good," Linda replied, looking disappointed. "I thought for sure they were going to go with the proposal I had put in front of them."

"And why did you think that was going to happen?" I asked.

"Because it made the most sense for their company," she replied after a brief pause. "The return-on-investment projections were very strong and we were addressing exactly what they wanted to achieve moving forward. And after all that I still cannot believe he asked me for something else that was less expensive."

"Why do you think he did that?" I asked.

"I don't know," replied Linda. "I guess the guy is just cheap and will never spend the money needed to get him to his goals."

This was the third sales meeting Linda had had with this same customer and each time he had indicated that he needed more time to think about it. In the end, Linda spent far too much time with this customer trying to close this deal. For instead of helping her make her month, it ended up being a waste of time for the order size received. But it didn't have to be this way.

Linda did many things right in this sale. She targeted a client that fit her ideal client avatar. She carried out her sales steps and activities well and even put forward the correct proposal for the customer. Despite doing all of these things well, though, she was missing one critical element in her sale. Linda did not help her customer answer the one question we all ask ourselves every time we buy: **COMPARED TO WHAT?**

Throughout our lives we all go through experiences that help influence the decisions we make moving forward—the more experiences we have, the better decisions we can make. This is why employers value experience so highly; they would prefer that the mistakes you learned come at somebody else's expense.

Our experiences also play into how we buy. It's human nature to want to improve upon a repetitive process, so naturally the more you buy, the better a buyer you can become. But for most people today, bigger buying decisions are an infrequent process and can come with a number of stresses based on the number of decisions and choices you have to choose from. As we discuss in this book, the right brain can quickly become paralyzed in the decision-making process when too many options and choices overwhelm our ability to decide to buy.

## THE CLOSING POWER OF DECISION SIMPLICITY

I recently worked with a division of a Fortune 500 company that sold more than 138 different products and services to the same customers. Not only were their different offerings difficult for their salespeople to sell, but they were hard for the customers to buy as well. **The most successful companies do the opposite and always strive to make their products and services easier to buy and easier to sell than their competition.**

Although the company had grown rapidly over the years, adding new products largely through acquisitions, little focus was given to how best to sell the ever-growing numbers of products and, as a result, their sales growth was largely stagnant. Every day their salespeople had to make far too many of their own choices about what to sell and in turn made their customers do the same when it came to buying. This is not dissimilar to what many people deal with when they go out to eat . . . especially around dinner time.

For example, when is the last time you looked at a wine list at a fancy restaurant? Or how about the many hundreds of different wines you can choose from at a grocery or liquor store? What is your initial reaction when you see this? Unless you are a raging alcoholic, most people are simply overwhelmed with the number of choices they see and either ask for a recommendation, buy a brand that is more familiar to them, or simply take the path of least resistance by ordering by the glass and not a whole bottle of wine at all. There are simply too many choices (intentionally or not), often leading to lower bottle sales of wine. We have seen this behavior in other consumables as well.

A perfect example comes from a study conducted in 2000 by psychologist Sheena Iyengar, who noticed that the grocery store she loved to frequent had hundreds of choices of many different items ranging from olive oils to jams. This isn't unusual since a typical grocery store today will have around 45,000 different items, while a Walmart can have more than 100,000. In this case, the aisle for jam alone provided customers with 348 different options. So this is where Sheena decided to start her study.

For her study, a jam-tasting table was set up near the entrance of the grocery store. One group of people passing by was provided with 24 different jams to taste while a second group was provided with only 6. The table with 24 options had a 60 percent visit rate versus only 40 percent for the table with 6 jams. However, the number of people who decided to buy after tasting the jams was only 6 percent for the table with 24 options versus 30 percent of buyers for the table with 6 jams. In summary, even though the initial traffic was higher to the table with more choices, the table with fewer choices yielded ten times the number of resulting sales.[1]

Now, back to the Fortune 500 company with 138 product/service choices and stagnant sales growth. In order to make their products and services easier to buy and sell, they decided to bundle some of their offerings into a limited number of new offerings that were sold together without the option of picking and choosing within the bundles. The result? An increase in annual sales of over 10 percent by doing nothing more than selling their existing products and services in a more efficient manner.

All of these issues come down to one thing called "decision simplicity." Recent studies have shown that **decision simplicity is now the number-one reason buyers decide to move forward with an intended purchase**. Decision simplicity was weighted against 40 other variables, including pricing and brand perception, and still finished on top. So when was the last time you heard a salesperson claim they lost a sale due to decision simplicity? You haven't, and you won't. In most cases, you will hear the 40 other reasons instead—the most common being price.[2]

This was the same reasoning Linda was using for her vastly diminished recent sale. But if Linda would look further, she would see that there are a number of things she could be doing differently that will drastically change her fortunes. Here are some of the main areas of improvement:

## CREATE BUNDLED SALES OPTIONS

If you've ever been to a fast-food restaurant you've seen the power of bundling in full force—ever heard of a Happy Meal? Many of these restaurants will offer up to 120 individual choices but will prominently display only seven combination meals. And for good reason: These businesses cannot afford to confuse their customers when they are ready to buy, for **a confused mind always says "no."** Psychologists refer to this confusion and anxiety as the "paradox of choice." Rather than confusion, velocity of sales and maximum utilization of resources are the name of the game for these restaurants, which is why they want consumers to limit their primary choices to no more than seven.

Now just imagine what these fast-food restaurants would be like today if all 120-plus menu items were displayed without bundled options. Instead of one choice, customers would have to make up to two or three additional choices in order to buy a simple meal. You would still see people standing around in this scenario—only this time it wouldn't be waiting after the order for their food was placed but rather while trying to decide on the order itself. McDonald's was one of the first fast-food restaurants to figure this out—starting nearly seven decades ago!

In 1948, the McDonald brothers shut down their already successful restaurant and reopened it after a remodeling of their business. **Before they shut down, McDonald's offered 25 menu items. After they reopened, they offered only 9.** Even though their initial goal may have been to increase quality and production time by focusing on the fewer items that constituted the vast majority of their sales, the McDonald brothers showed the power of Sheena Iyengar's jam study in action—over 50 years before she proved it once again.

Many bigger businesses have caught on to the power of bundling and it's hard to buy anything now—ranging from software, automobiles, music, etc.—without being presented with a bundled option. The more options you provide your sellers and buyers (think of the jam study), the more valuable selling bundled options can be for your business.

## DEFINE YOUR CUSTOMER'S CHOICES FOR THEM

Last year I took my car in for an oil change at a local automotive tire and service shop. What started out as a simple $29 oil change quickly turned into a series of potential upsells ranging from the flushing of my coolant system to the quality of my brake fluid. Sound familiar? I've been through this dog and pony show so many times that it can be hard to say "yes" or "no" when asked—especially if you don't really know anything about cars beyond simply driving them.

During my visit, the mechanic working on my car came into the waiting room and showed me the results of a test he had performed on my brake fluid. The first chart showed the color of my brake fluid (lighter is good, darker is bad) and what percentage of moisture was in my brake fluid (higher levels of moisture is bad). Now, before we go any further with this story, there are a few more details we need to know about brake fluid here.

First, brake fluid is hygroscopic, meaning it likes to attract moisture. Second, the more moisture that gets in your brake fluid, the lower the boiling point of the brake fluid. Third, if the boiling point is too low, your car can suffer from pedal fade, brake failure, and corrosion and therefore replacement of brake lines and calipers. Fourth, all of this can help attribute to the 10,000 brake-failure related accidents that happen each year in the United States.[3] Now back to our mechanic salesman.

When the mechanic showed me the comparisons of what good brake fluid looks like and the acceptable moisture content compared to mine, he had my attention. He also had my attention when he said a replacement would cost $129 to complete—which was four times the cost of my original oil change. The mechanic was trained well enough in providing me with a comparison of good and bad, but I had one more choice as well—I could simply say "no," which is what I did that day. He was a mechanic and not a salesman so he was not offended. I, on the other hand, wanted to learn more.

Shortly after my auto service upsell experience, I called up my friend Bill, who owns a larger automotive service shop with around eight full-time mechanics working during regular business hours. I discussed my experience with the previous service shop and he explained that in his business, cheap oil changes are largely not profitable for shops but rather serve as loss-leaders to help get people in so they can then provide upsell opportunities to those additional services that are highly profitable. Of all these various services offered, he claimed that brake fluid changes are one of his highest margin services and he encourages his mechanics to pursue them when needed. The only problem was who was pursuing them and how well.

When I asked Bill to run a six-month report on the various upsell services provided, including brake fluid changes, I asked him to include the mechanic's name next to each one. After sorting through the list, I found that one mechanic (out of eight total) in particular had sold nearly 50 percent of all the brake fluid services over the past six months. When I asked Bill if this mechanic received a higher number of these types of services, he said no, explaining that all services are on a random rotation unless requested by the car owner.

Wanting to know more, I then decided to listen to all eight mechanics go through their typical brake fluid upsell pitches that Bill had taught them. All of them were the same except for one: the mechanic who sold nearly 50 percent of all of the brake fluid changes over the past six months. After I completed my reviews, I went back to Bill with my results.

"Bill, you said you train your mechanics to test the visual quality and moisture content of each customer's brake fluid and present those results compared to what is ideal," I said. "You also told me that most people will refuse this service after the price is presented—even if the service is needed. But you have one mechanic who does this differently and it just happens to be the one selling more of this high-margin service than anybody else."

"So what is he doing differently?" responded Bill with an inquisitive look on his face.

"Bill, the reason he is so successful in selling this service compared to the other mechanics is because he clearly articulates the choices and the value of inaction to the customer in such an effective way that most people weigh the opportunity cost as being insignificant compared to the $129 needed to help prevent it," I said.

"So how does he do that?" asked Bill.

"Simple," I said. "Most people know the value of their own money and they don't expect to pay four times an expected service price to fix a potential problem they were previously unaware of. So this one mechanic starts his pitch by first indicating that he did his checks on their car and then asks the customer if they ever notice any pedal fade or trouble braking from time to time when they drive."

Now, it's important to point out that most people do not think their car ever brakes perfectly because they don't drive enough other cars to know the difference. Nor do they know what "pedal fade" really is. So when a mechanic asks this type of question, most people will become curious and want to know more—especially when the question is asked in a way that may indicate a potential problem may exist.

"By asking this question, he makes your customers curious and they start asking him questions in return," I said. "At this point, your mechanic will tell his customers that the NHTSA (National Highway & Traffic Safety Administration) tracks around 10,000 brake-failure related auto accidents each year; many of which could have been prevented through simple maintenance. At this point, your customers will ask him, 'What kind of simple maintenance?' to which he will then explain the potential dangers of their current brake fluid condition and how he can help fix it now before it gets any worse."

Bill sat back in his seat and started taking notes—clearly he wanted his other mechanics to use this same upsell strategy and help increase his profits. He then looked up and asked me, "Do you think my other mechanics can do this same thing?"

"Of course they can," I responded. "But first you need to teach them the importance of providing choices, value, and costs associated to each potential decision their customers have to make in their own minds. Once your mechanics understand why this is so important, how they do it can become much more effective."

The world today is full of buying choices, whether they're as simple as which bottled water to buy when you're thirsty or as complicated as which home to buy when you want to own a place to live. Despite the number of choices, **consumers will typically give more time and thought to the choices they have to make when the price of their purchases increase.**

Whether you know it or not, at least 25 percent of consumers who make purchasing decisions of greater that $50 indicate that most of their effort in the sales process is around product research—while 20 percent indicate it's around comparison shopping.[4] If you have a sale that seems to drag on or go quiet, it could very well fall into one of these two buckets.

One of the biggest mistakes salespeople make is letting potential customers discover their choices all on their own. When left to do this on their own, your customers will have three options. First, they can decide to move forward with you—which you have the greatest chance of closing if you are the first choice presented to them. Second, they can research other options and competitors and try to determine which one is best for them. Or third, they can procrastinate or become overwhelmed with the decision-making process and make the easiest decision of all—which is to do nothing. Doing nothing is where most decisions end up.

**When it comes to buying, people need a frame of reference to help them know if the choice they make is the right choice to make. The more unfamiliar people are with their choices, the more significant this comparative analysis becomes in the buyer's mind.** For example, when I decide to go out to eat, I have many choices but I will quickly decide on the location I wish to eat at based on the options that are most familiar to me—which comes from eating out often. If, however, I decide that I want to buy a new TV for my house, which I do much more infrequently than eating out, I will research and consider a number of choices before I decide to buy—the bigger the purchase, the more time and research I will commit to this process. Your customers do the same thing every day, and there are ways to make this work to your advantage.

The first thing you need to know is that too many choices will quickly lead your customers to information overload and no decision to buy. Conversely, getting a buyer down to one product/service is really getting them down to two choices: you or no decision at all. If you leave your customer alone to successfully vet all of their other choices, most will not and leave you with no decision. Finally, no matter where you are in the sales process, the easiest decision that anybody can make and the decision that we are all well trained to make is to make no decision at all. Do you see the point here? **You will ALWAYS have at least one** competitor (doing nothing) with anything you sell and it will always be the easiest and most formidable competitor you will ever face in anything you ever sell.

The second point you need to remember is that your customers want a trusted advisor when they need help buying and making choices—and most people don't inherently trust salespeople. That's why referrals are the lifeblood of many successful salespeople and businesses. Therefore, it is important for you to set yourself apart from other salespeople by offering your customers more support in making an informed decision—with your help, of course.

The third point to remember is that comparisons are relative to each individual's perspective. For example, many people know that actor Tom Selleck is tall at 6'4". But if you have him stand next to NBA stars Yao Ming (7'6") and Shawn Bradley (7'6"), he will appear shorter in comparison. Ever wondered why car dealers sometimes put their most expensive cars up front—making them the first cars and prices people see when entering their stores? Companies that sell on quality over price often do the same thing. Psychologists refer to this as the "contrast principle," and we see it in use every day—even if you aren't looking . . . or are just eating dinner.

For example, when working in New York City, one of my favorite restaurants was the Waverly Inn. In addition to a live tree growing through the ceiling of their restaurant, they also had another comparative uniqueness on their menu. For a mere $95, you could order the most expensive dish of truffle mac and cheese in New York City. Now, most people, including myself, did not order this insanely expensive dish. It wasn't so much about the price for me as it was that I hate truffle oil and continue to be repulsed by restaurants that unnecessarily ruin perfectly good dishes by adding truffle oil to them so they can sell them for a higher price.

Despite my personal tastes, this overpriced menu item was brilliant for a number of reasons. First, it created a unique signature option for this restaurant that people fondly remembered and freely talked about. Second, by having such a premium item on the menu, it suggested to customers that the overall quality of ALL of the food offered was high. And finally, since many people noticed the expensive truffle mac and cheese item first, everything else on the menu seemed "more affordable" by comparison.

The fourth point to remember is that you should provide your customers with all of the most common comparisons (including doing nothing) so they can better understand your unique value, their opportunity costs, and why they should choose you over any potential competition. Some companies will provide this in a chart with a comparative product matrix while others will create a more customized proposal that is better tailored to a specific customer.

When creating these comparative options in sales, remember the technique used by fast-food restaurants. We know that they try to limit their combination meal options to seven choices or less. They can do this because most people are generally familiar with these options due to their own experiences buying at these restaurants in the past. In sales, especially when selling higher-priced products and services, consumer buying experience tends to be much more limited, and therefore fewer options are typically needed—with no more than three options being ideal in many industries today.

When presented with three buying options, most people tend to gravitate to the middle option—which you can make work to your advantage. For example, if your first option is the opportunity cost of doing nothing, then your third option can be your truffle mac and cheese dish—which, ideally, is designed to be more expensive to make your second (middle) option seem more reasonable in comparison. Just be careful not to pick your third option as something so outrageous that your buyers would never consider it at any cost. Rather, it should be something they would want the most if pricing was not a major consideration.

But not every choice we make is about making a direct buying decision. When it comes to making other choices the same principle of limited choices still applies. For example, consumer reviews online have recently become all the rage and many websites now ask consumers to rate various companies, products, and/or services based on a five-star rating system with an additional sixth option to add personalized comments. The only problem with this is that the average business rating received online today is a 4.3—which leaves most consumers to wonder if that rating is good or bad and, more important, compared to what? Moreover, do people really believe that a business, product, or service with a perfect rating of five stars provided by many different users is really accurate and trustworthy?[5]

This inability for consumers to distinguish the true comparative value of these ratings has resulted in recent changes in the number of choices provided by consumer review systems alone. For example, Netflix recently tested a change in their ratings system by moving from a five-star-plus-comments model (six total choices) to a simpler thumbs-up or thumbs-down option (two options). The result was a 100 percent increase in the participation rates of users providing reviews. Moreover, Netflix also claimed that this new limited-review model resulted in people being more honest with their reviews as well.[6]

It is also important to understand that even if you really only have one option to provide (which is still two choices if they decide not to buy), you don't have to limit your options to only your own offerings. If you have one or two major competitors, you can use their products and services in your own comparative process as well. If you find that your sales prospects are already doing this, find out who they will alternatively consider on their own and who they will consider the most compared to you. You can then arm your customers with the information they need to make a more informed decision, with your help—leading to higher levels of trust and sales.

## REFRAME THE BUYING OF VALUE

Have you ever wondered why nearly all businesses today take credit cards, knowing that they have to pay an additional transaction fee to the banks of 3 to 5 percent instead of simply saving that money by taking only cash? They do this because **many businesses and banks know that people will spend around 15 to 30 percent more on purchases**

**using their credit cards compared to cash.**[7] This is one of the reasons I advise people who are trying to get out of debt to pay for everything in cash and see what happens to their spending behaviors. But banks and credit card companies are not the only ones to put this convenience of buying with credit cards to work for them.

Think about the following question: Would you be more or less willing to buy something for $36,000 now compared to paying $567 a month over 60 months instead for the same thing? This is the same the question that millions of average Americans face each year when they decide to purchase an automobile. Can you imagine what would happen to automobile sales if people could only pay in cash and had to pay in full at the time of the transaction? Naturally new car sales would plummet. So why do so many companies and salespeople still operate in a similar manner?

In sales, you may have little or no say in what you sell but you may have many options in how you can sell it. For example, will you take a steady stream of payments from those customers who are less willing to pay up front? Do you provide an option to pay by credit card versus cash? Or can you offer a delay in the initial payments from your customers in order to get them to buy from you now? All of these are examples of ways in which other successful salespeople and companies have made the selling and buying process more effective and less painful.

Even though we see many major businesses like car dealers, furniture stores, and the like adopt the reframing of value in payments, I am still amazed at how many other businesses still don't—most common of which are smaller- to medium-sized businesses who just so happen to also have the highest failure rates. One such example came from a recent experience I had when I needed a new water softening system for my home.

Now, for those who don't know much about soft water systems, in Arizona you have to learn quickly since we have some of the hardest water in the country. Not initially knowing much about these systems, I first reverted to familiarity and we contacted two of the most recogniz-able names in the business to see how much it cost to "purchase" a new water softening system for our home. Of the options presented, we decided that the higher-end model that contained both the softening and carbon filtering was the one we wanted. That was until we were quoted the prices. Ouch!

Both of the options installed would cost us around $5,000—clearly thousands more than we initially expected to pay for these systems. Upon this discovery, I quickly turned to the Internet and found an unfamiliar company with a comparatively large amount of consumer reviews. Upon further research, I also discovered that this company provided another alternative to buying a new system outright. Their model was for customers to rent an equivalent system, including all service warranties and a five-year equipment upgrade plan, all for $50 dollars a month. To make my decision even easier, the installation costs were later waived on credit after providing them with a few positive reviews online and, best of all, there were no contract commitments—the service was month-to-month and I could cancel at any time.

When I met the owner of this company (Boyett's Family Rayne Water Conditioning), I wanted to learn more about his business. As it turns out, I quickly learned that the equipment used in the process of water softening is rather fungible and short of a few technological niceties that were lost on me, the quality differences were largely moot. At that point, the decision then came down to the two other pillars to compete on—service and price—and on both fronts they won hands down.

Now, some may argue that I made a mistake in renting and not purchasing a new system, and they could be right. But after owning and maintaining one of these systems in the past, I was much more comfortable with this rental option over eight years compared to the cost of recovering that same amount of money by buying and owning from someone else over the same period of time. More important, the value of "doing nothing" versus buying a new system for $5,000 was far more compelling for my wife and me—until I was presented with a much easier and more convenient way to buy by renting instead.

The end result of softer water was the same for our family, so why not make the comparatively easier buying decision? To no surprise of my own, this rental company has now become one of the largest water softening companies in Arizona and according to the owner has steadily grown around 10 percent each year over the past two decades alone. Are the products they offer superior to their competition? Many would argue that they are largely the same. Some could even argue that their services are similar as well. But when it comes time to buy, they have the clearest competitive advantage of all. If you run a small business, you can learn a lot from this company!

Although changes in payment options can be effective, you can also help reframe the description of these payment options to an even greater effect. A recent study out of Carnegie Mellon University showed how a simple change of wording alone can have a significant impact on buying decisions. In this study, researchers changed the description of an over-night shipping charge added to a free DVD trial offer from "a $5 fee" to "a small $5 fee," resulting in a 20 percent increase in orders.[8]

If you ever watch TV, you will see this descriptive reframing used all the time and to great effect. For example, reframing phrases commonly used include "low monthly payments," "for the low-low price of . . . " "for only . . . " etc. Or how about those products that are offered for "three easy payments of just $19.99"? Not only does this reframe the immediate pricing but also the relative size of it—even if you and I know there is no such thing as an easy payment. In these semantical changes we find effective ways in which a relative descriptive change by wording alone is provided, which some buyers will respond favorably to . . . simply because you helped answered the question "compared to what?" in the minds of your buyers.

## USE RECIPROCITY TO HELP CREATE DISTINCTION

Shortly after I opened my first checking account with First National Bank of Omaha, I was like most young people of my day and would frequent the drive-through ATM to withdraw cash to help fund my youthful bliss. I didn't want to carry too much money with me at any one time for to do so would bring back the haunting advice of my grandfather, who would tell me that having too much money with me "will burn a hole in your pocket."

So one weekend when the bank was closed I decided to visit the bank's 24/7 ATM to withdraw cash. The only problem was that the bank ATM was not functioning properly that day and gave me an error screen upon my attempted withdrawal. So that day I went without cash and, yes, I somehow managed to survive. But what happened a week later I will never forget for the rest of my life.

Upon opening my mail, I noticed an envelope from First National Bank of Omaha enclosed with an apology letter for the malfunction of their ATM and a $5 bill to help make amends. Had I not moved away from Omaha a few years later, I would certainly have remained a loyal customer for life—all because of a simple $5 bill I unexpectedly received from them decades ago.

**One of the first lessons I instill in salespeople is that you have to learn and practice how to give in order to receive.** Certainly some will associate religious connotations to such a belief, but no matter your perspective on life, reciprocity is one of the most powerful tools you have in dealing with other people. In the business word, this is especially so. But giving also can come with limitations.

Giving should not be confused with direct selling, which is where many salespeople can get into trouble. Giving materially in direct return for an action is considered unethical in many industries and, depending on the extent of the give, can also be considered a bribe. In sales, giving should ideally be part of the relationship-building process and not directly tied to a specific business transaction.

There are three key aspects to making giving an effective part of your customer relationships. First, **giving should be unique and unexpected.** One of my favorite memories growing up as a young child was watching my father send out Thanksgiving Day letters each year to all of his contacts, both personal and professional. Each year he would write a highly personalized letter about the past year and what he was thankful for. We children would then help him fold, address, stamp, and lick the envelopes for the thousands of letters that went out each year. One year when my father's health was failing he did not send out the letters, and what followed was truly amazing. Many of the people who had previously received his letters reached out to find out what was wrong and to let us know that his letters were one of the things they looked forward to most during the holiday season.

What this experience taught me about giving was that the best way to give is not to follow the sheep but to be creative and stand out from the crowd. Think about it: What do most people do around the Christmas holiday? They give Christmas gifts and cards. Remember the famous scene from the movie *National Lampoon's Christmas Vacation* when Clark Griswold brings in a gift for his boss and the reaction he received? Not only was his gift nearly identical to the other gifts on the table, but his boss's reaction was to tell him to "put it over there with the others." Now, what if Clark Griswold were to have provided a different gift to his boss at a time of year when nobody else provided one? What do you suppose his boss's reaction would have been then and, more important, what sense of obligation would that have created?

There are many ways to give but, like most people, we tend to give like lemmings; which is why you should always strive to be different. Giving can be beneficial at any time if done tastefully and unexpectedly, **so always shoot for the unexpected and give when others typically don't.** When starting a relationship, don't be afraid to give free initial advice if they aren't expecting it. When thanking a customer, give in a way and at a time they do not expect from other businesses and professionals. When speaking and publishing information, don't be afraid to give useful information in a way your audience wouldn't initially expect, such as a discount on services for mentioning your speech, etc.

Second, **the best giving is personalized giving.** Say you receive two letters of congratulations from two highly esteemed people in your profession; one is handwritten and the other is typed. Which one means more to you? Which one will you remember the most? If the answer is so obvious to most people then why is it that most of us will not send out handwritten letters?

One of my favorite stories about personalized giving comes from one of my favorite salespeople of all time: Joe Girard—the World's Greatest Car Salesman. Over the course of twelve years, Joe sold 13,000 cars. That works out to 6 cars sold a day when the average car salesman sold 5 a month. Joe gave out 16,000 "uniquely designed" business cards per month when the average salesperson gave out 500 standard ones. Joe gave out $50 referral fees (around $200 dollars in 2017 dollars) for new customer referrals when most other salespeople paid nothing. Joe constantly asked for referrals when only 11 percent of salespeople ever do. And most important, Joe learned about and appreciated his clients and wrote each one of them a handwritten, personalized note each month when the average car salesman did not. And what were the results of all these efforts? Nearly 70 percent of Joe's customers were repeat customers or came from people they knew.[9]

Giving in order to receive can also take time, **so be patient;** your returns may not be immediate but will pay off over time. When I was in Boy Scouts, we had a simple motto: "Do a good deed every day." In sales, you should have a similar motto: **"Give a good deed every day."** Watch what happens to your results. Remember, people will only respond to your prospecting efforts through a sense of curiosity, obligation, and urgency. It feels good to most people to give to others and it can feel even better when your prospective customers give back in return.

Giving applies to marketing as well. Many businesses today will use giving as a way to help grow awareness and usage of their services. For example, Uber recently offered a "Get Free Rides" promotion to in effect turn their current customers into marketing agents for their company. In this case, the Uber app allowed current customers to invite non-users to try Uber and become new Uber customers. When the recipient received the invite, their first ride with Uber was free (up to $20). Once they used the offer, the current customer who invited them also received the same $20 deal. Uber knows that the average lifetime value of a new customer should far exceed these initial costs and uses this promotion as a very effective loss leader in generating new customer growth.

Moreover, by giving to both their current and future customers to help grow their customer base, everybody wins.

Giving can be seen to one degree or another in nearly all industries today—and it works! Those free samples you receive at the stores, those free mailing labels you receive unsolicited in the mail, those free meals you receive from your customers, and those free drink coupons I regularly receive from Southwest Airlines for helping them keep their planes flying a lot are all signs of reciprocity.

In the end reciprocity works because we are all human and, as such, **we have a natural tendency to want to return favors and repay in kind to those who have provided to us.** In sales, reciprocity also helps to tear down the walls many people instinctively put up around salespeople and helps curb their instinct to repulse from more complex sales transactions.

# CHAPTER 11

# PEOPLE WHO TELL STORIES RULE THE WORLD

• • •

*"People who tell stories rule the world."*
— *PLATO*

It was perhaps one of the most painful sales meetings I had been to in months. Linda pulled out her PowerPoint, which was densely packed full of company-provided text, talking points, and materials that screamed "You are being sold" and "I am wasting my time" to anybody watching. It was hard to watch and would have put anybody to sleep—including my children, who can stay awake through seemingly anything. But I've seen this dog and pony show many times before.

As the sales meeting went on and on, I could see the potential customer, Andy, deflating like an old balloon right in front of my eyes. His body was starting to slouch in his chair, his eyelids growing heavier, his arms crossed, and his eyes wandering off at anything and everything around him—especially his watch. Nearly twenty minutes had now passed and Linda was losing the sale right in front of my eyes. I had to stop the bleeding before it got any worse.

"Andy, can I ask you a question?" I said as I broke into the presentation.

"Sure," Andy responded as he tried to pull himself out of the mental fog he was now in.

"When we started you had mentioned that your customers don't find services like yours through the Internet or on social media, right?" I asked.

"That's right," Andy responded.

"And you said because of that you don't need things like websites and social media to help generate new customers, right?" I continued.

"That's right," Andy responded again.

"I can totally understand why you feel that way. I would feel the same way if were in your shoes," I responded. "You know Gerald Young, right? He's also in your line of work."

"Sure, I know Gerald," Andy replied.

"Well so do I," I said. "In fact, Gerald told me the exact same thing you just told me over a year ago, and then he lost one of his biggest potential customers ever. Did Gerald ever tell you the story about why that happened?"

"No," replied Andy. At this point I clearly had Andy's fully attention.

"I met with Gerald over a year ago and he told me that he didn't need a website or social media since all of his clients come from referrals," I said. "He said if they wanted to learn anything about him they could simply Google his name and see all his news—and he was right. As you know, Gerald is constantly in the news due to having high-profile customers just like yours. Because of that, Gerald told me the same thing you just told me—until the first day of January."

"What happened in January?" Andy asked while leaning forward and paying close attention.

"I received a phone call on January first from Gerald, who told me, 'Get your ass in here now—we need to talk!'" I said. "So I proceeded to his office that afternoon. Once I arrived, Gerald said we needed to get started now with a website, social media, everything—all the services we had discussed nearly six months earlier. With a rather perplexed look on my face, I then asked Gerald, 'So what happened since the last time we talked that changed your mind?'

"'I just lost my biggest potential customer ever,' said Gerald, looking down while pointing at the front cover of the newspaper on his desk. 'You probably know about this guy because he's been all over the news for the past few weeks. He was a referral and we had a great initial meeting and then everything went quiet—not a word from him since.

Well, I ran into him last night at a New Year's party and when I asked him why he didn't use me, he said that our meeting went well, as did his meetings with the other two referrals he received. The problem was that after the meetings, he looked us all up online and since I was the only one without a website and social media, he thought that meant that I was not 'up to date' on my business. So I lost the damn customer and you are going to help me make sure that doesn't happen to me ever again.'"

Andy sat back in his seat, nodding his head, and for the first time since our meeting began, Andy started to smile. Linda, who was sitting beside me, also started to smile.

After a brief pause Andy said, "So what you're trying to tell me is that if I don't use your services, I could lose big customers just like Gerald did?"

"That is exactly what Gerald would tell you based on his own experience and why we are here today to help you," I responded.

The meeting proceeded from there and Andy ended up signing a contract thirty minutes later. But without the story, the sale was dead on arrival.

## THE HISTORY OF STORYTELLING

Long before smart phones, the Internet, books, and even the written word, man used stories to entertain, teach, and pass on knowledge to others. All throughout history, humans had to rely on their memories to teach and learn through stories. As groups of people began to form together to live in tribes and clans, the storyteller became a person of increasing importance, respect, and power among their people.

Great storytellers in history include such names as Homer, Jesus, Shakespeare, Abraham Lincoln, and many others who preceded and followed them. All of them had a profound impact on civilization and frequently thought and communicated with others through stories.

Why?

**Because humans are programmed to think and learn through the use of stories—it is literally in our DNA.** Stories are so effective because they mirror human thinking patterns and provide form, context, and facts for human thought. We tend to learn best from others through stories because as listeners we become emotionally engaged and therefore better remember what we hear.

Instead of stories, many salespeople today use facts. But facts are most effective in a sales process only if they can help conceptualize a message—typically by telling a story. Without a basis to support a fact in the mind of the customer, it only leads to annoyance and confusion, and a confused mind always says "no."

Storytelling is powerful because it also provides meaning and relevance to information, and **people cannot remember anything without giving it meaning.** Think about it: If I were to say four numbers to you, would you remember them in order? Most people would quickly forget because even though they may know the four numbers provided they cannot associate a particular meaning to them. If, however, I told you I had the four numbers that make up the password to your bank debit card, I would then have your attention since the numbers now have meaning to you. This is also why **stories are memorable and statistics are not.** Studies have shown that after a sales presentation, 63 percent of the attendees remember the stories told while only 5 percent remember the statistics.[1]

A sales process is in effect an attempt to teach and get others to change. Therefore the ultimate decision to buy is a decision first made in the emotional brain and later rationalized by the logical brain. **Without the emotion gained through the use of stories, you are only selling based largely on logic to the part of the brain that does not send the initial signals to buy.** This is where so many salespeople fail in selling—for they try to connect and sell at the rational level, which in most cases is not compelling enough to get others to want to change. The people you are selling to may be able to understand and rationalize what you're selling based on logic alone but they will not be emotionally compelled to move forward and say "yes" unless you use stories to help them make this connection.

# HOW TO STRUCTURE SALES STORIES

Now that you know the importance of storytelling in sales, the next step is to know what type of stories you will need and how to use them to produce the best results. But let's start by testing just how much you really know about stories.

What do the movies *Star Wars, The Lord of the Rings, The Lion King, The Wizard of Oz, Dances with Wolves, The Hunger Games,* and *Rocky* all have in common? If you said they were some of the most popular movies of all time you would be right. But did you also know that all of these movies were based on the same type of story called the hero's journey?

"The hero's journey" is the basis for many of the greatest books and movies ever made. The hero's journey is based on a person (the hero) who from their ordinary world is called to adventure. During their journey, they meet their mentor, who helps them through their struggles, transformation, atonement, and ultimately their changed return.

Now, unlike with a great movie, most people will not give you two hours of their time to listen to a story of this length, but there are many different structures you can use to present this journey in a way that will help you sell more effectively. As a result, many of the most successful sales stories are structured in three distinct elements: **The setup/setting,** which is how the world once was for the hero (the buyer) before a change; **the confrontation/conflict,** where the hero struggles; and **the resolution/transformation,** where the hero and/or the world around him has changed—preferably through the help of you as their mentor (the trusted sales advisor).

In the example story I used at the beginning of this chapter, you can clearly see these elements in use: The customer, Gerald (the hero), did not want to change by purchasing a new website and social media from us **(the setup/setting).** Only when Gerald had lost his prized potential customer **(the confrontation/conflict)** did he decide that he needed my help **(the mentor)** to build him a new website and social media presence so he would never lose another marquee prospective customer like this again **(the resolution/transformation).** By presenting this story to my sales prospect Andy, he was then better able to relate to Gerald and see the same possible transformation in his own world and was therefore better able to justify the journey and change in his own mind.

Most sales stories can be effectively told with this type of structure and in a way that will help abbreviate any two-hour movie/story into a two-to-four-minute *sales* story. Remember: Sales stories can be highly effective but must be timely as well. Shakespeare said it best: "Brevity is the soul of wit."

## START YOUR SALES STORIES ON A HIGH NOTE

Stories are presented in many different ways throughout the sales and marketing process. **In sales, most people will make a decision of "attention" or "no-attention" within the first 20–30 seconds you engage them.**[2] In sales situations where you are using stories with cold-audience prospects who you have not yet developed a level of trust with, most are not going to patiently wait for you to build up your story over the course of 2–4 minutes.

Because of this, **most "cold audience" stories should start out at the highest level of suspense**—which is typically around the middle of the story where the confrontation/conflict are at the highest. Going back to the story at the beginning of this chapter, notice how I started off by initially talking about how Gerald had just lost his largest potential customer. This was clearly designed to create a high level of suspense during the transformation to the story so Andy would be curious enough to want to listen to the rest.

When you start a story out at the initial point of suspense, you can then walk the customer back to the beginning of the full story (or backstory) once you've grabbed their attention and curiosity—as I showed above when asking Andy if he had heard the full story about Gerald's loss.

Hitting the point of suspense in selling by stories also applies to other forms of sales and marketing. Unlike personal meetings where you may have 20–30 seconds to grab a prospective customer's attention, you will typically receive far less time when using emails, letters, phone calls, etc. Because of this, you want to be most effective by calling out your point of suspense right way. This is why subject lines in emails, headlines in articles, and introductions over the phone are so critical to get right when selling with stories.

Let's use the subject line of an email for example. Studies have shown that **64 percent of people indicate that they will decide whether or not to open an email based on the subject line alone.**[3] If I were to use Gerald's story in an email, which of the following subject lines do you think would be most effective in getting people's attention and piquing their curiosity enough to want to read the rest of my story and email?

1. Gerald didn't want a website (Setup/Setting)

2. Gerald just lost his biggest potential customer ever (Confrontation/ Conflict)

3. Gerald bought a website from me (Resolution/Transformation)

If you answered with the second option—Gerald just lost his biggest potential customer ever—you would be right. Again, we are using the confrontation/conflict and throwing it right out in front of people as a grabber. It's also important to remember that people are not perfect and therefore cannot relate to stories of other perfect people. By understanding this element of human nature, any conflict/struggle is most effective in initially grabbing people's attention—especially if the recipients potentially share the same types of struggles in their own lives as we saw above with Gerald and Andy.

## THE STORIES YOU NEED TO CREATE

Now that you know how to properly structure a sales story, the next question is what type of stories you need to create. There are a number of stories you can use based on your respective sales processes, but the best stories are those that help address the "Five Whys of Closing" we discussed in chapter 9. These stories include:

**Customer introduction stories** about your own journey and that of your organization. These stories help you get past the **"why you"** and "why your company" concerns that are initially on the minds of your customers. People want to buy from people they like and organizations they respect but most important of all, they do not want to buy "what" you're selling but rather "why" you're selling it.

In these stories, you and the company are the "hero"—but don't misconstrue that for meaning you are perfect and never make mistakes. **People are not interested in stories about perfect people and/or organizations. Not only do they not exist in real life but people cannot relate to them.** For this reason, do not be afraid to lower your guard and admit flaws—people will empathize, respect, and better relate to you for it. So why, then, are potential character flaws so important when telling a story?

Back in the 1980s one of the most popular TV series was *Magnum, P.I.,* which ran for eight years—and many more as reruns to follow. The star of the show was Thomas Magnum, played by Tom Selleck. At the time of casting for the show, Tom Selleck was not yet a household name and was coming off of six consecutive failed pilots. Selleck originally rejected the pilot, claiming that the character of Thomas Magnum was overly macho, heroic, and too perfect. According to Selleck, he "wanted the guy [Magnum] to make mistakes, to have flaws."[4]

The result was a TV series hit that propelled Tom Selleck to star status in Hollywood—in large part because Selleck insisted that his lead character have flaws. Clearly this worked, and illustrated just how important having flaws is in allowing people to better connect with others. As a result, viewers were clearly entertained by and fell in love with the flawed character of Thomas Magnum. Think about your flaws and the flaws of your company and write them down. The closer these flaws can relate to the flaws of your customers, the greater the emotional connection you can make by using them.

Your "why you" and "why your company" story will commonly tell your customers about your journey and how you got to this point and why. In many cases, these two stories can be combined into one journey story as well. Here is a good example of just such a story I've heard others use before: "Mr. Customer, I know you don't know me from a hole in the wall, and that's okay—I would feel the same way. My customers tell me the reason they like working with me is that I am always honest with them, I always look out for their success before mine, and they trust me. Now, I have worked with other companies in the past that didn't allow me to operate in this manner, so I left and ultimately ended up working here, where my ethics and that of the company are now aligned. Now, do my company and I still occasionally make mistakes? Of course we do—all businesses operate that way. But the difference is I will always look out for the best interests of my customers, and my current company operates in the same manner. That is why I'm here today, and that is my promise to you."

**The times I have found the use of "why you" and "why your company" stories most useful are usually toward the beginning of a customer sales meeting.** This allows you to immediately build credibility and call out the "elephant in the room" before your customers' brains go into defense mode and decide to tune you out while thinking that they are being "sold."

**In-common customer success stories** are your second and perhaps most important type of story you can use in selling. Why? **Because nothing arms salespeople to sell better than happy customers—and the best way to convey those successes are through stories.** These stories help you get past the **"why change"** and **"why your product/ service"** questions that are in the minds of your customers.

"Why change" stories must precede your "why your product" stories because without first overcoming the fear of change in the customers' minds, they will never be compelled to buy your product or service as a result—even if their current alternative of "doing nothing" is still not ideal. The old saying that "the devil you know is better than the devil you don't" clearly illustrates the fear of the unknown in the minds of your potential customers.

Because of this fear, your biggest competition is always to "do nothing," which is why up to **60 percent of sales end in no decision.**[5] So the goal with your "why change" stories should be to **help address this fear in your customers' minds by making the unknown known to them.**

In order to create your "why change" stories, you need to start by fully understanding the opportunity cost of inaction for your prospective customers. In other words, what is "doing nothing" costing them now versus what they could save/gain by taking action? This is where the importance of value and the value exchange comes in as it relates to money.

Your customers understand the value of one thing when you walk in the door: the value of their own money. Your goal, then, is to compel them (why change) to part with their money, ideally in exchange for your products/services (why your products/services). The only way to consistently do this is to more clearly communicate and provide a measure of value that they could receive from your products and services that exceeds the value of their money—the higher the value, the more likely they will be to buy.

But when you sell services, this value can be much harder to sell. Why? Because a product sale is nothing more than a simple value exchange: I provide you something of value (product) in return for something of value from you (money). A simple value exchange is immediate and intuitive; I buy something of value in exchange for an equal or lesser value in payment. When the value of what I buy is of less perceived value to me than the cost, I will either ask for a lower price to better reflect the perceived value exchange or simply not buy altogether. Conversely, if what I want to buy is of higher perceived value than the price, I will likely buy it now and perhaps in greater quantities to account for any potential correction in future prices. These concepts are simple supply and demand.

Where the value exchange becomes more complicated is when it's applied to the sale of services—especially those services provided by most salespeople today. Why? There are two primary reasons for this. First, most services today are intangible and inconsistent and therefore harder to accurately value until after the services have been fully delivered. Second, payments for professional services are commonly paid in part or in full in advance of the services rendered, creating a delayed exchange. A delayed exchange is the process of providing a standard of known value (commonly in money) for value (services) to be provided after the initial exchange takes place.

What makes delayed exchanges different from simple value exchanges is that **delayed exchanges only work based on a level of TRUST.** And one of the most effective ways to earn trust with others is to tell in-common stories about other customers who were in similar situations and how and why they successfully changed to your products/services.

Here is an example of how a "why change" and "why your products/services" story could look: "Mr. Customer, you just told me that your team of 150 salespeople are only spending around 40 percent of their time actually selling. That means that nearly 60 percent of their time is spent NOT directly generating sales for your company. I know you've heard of XYZ Company—they are in the same business as yours. Well, I met with XYZ Company nearly a year ago and they told me they had the same problem. It has been nine months since I started working with them and during our last meeting they indicated to me that our new system has increased the selling time of their salespeople by 38 percent, resulting in a projected increase of sales this year of $38.8 million. Their return on investment by changing how they sell is well in excess of 16 to 1, which most companies in your business would love to achieve. That is what I am offering you here today."

So ask yourself, if you were the customer in the example above and were told this story, how much more trust would you then have in the salesperson through the use of this story? Moreover, how much does the cost of "no change" now mean to you and your company?

When creating in-common customer success stories, **the goal should be to create as many stories as possible to closely match as many of your similar sales prospects' situations as possible.** The more customer success stories you can create and use, the more effective you will become when selling.

**Common customer objection stories** are your third set of stories and are primarily focused on helping you overcome sales objections. **The goal here is to think of all of the most common rejections you**

receive when selling and assign a journey story for each to help you overcome them. These stories will also help you get past the "why now" questions that are in the minds of your customers. It's important to remember that **"why now"** objection questions typically come around the critical time of the close, which means your **"why now" stories should have a strong emotional call-to-action element** that most appeals to the portion of the brain that sends the signal to the buyer to say "yes."

Let's use the story we just discussed and apply it to a very common "price" objection: "Mr. Customer, you just told me that our system is too expensive. You also told me that your team of 150 salespeople are only spending around 40 percent of their time actually selling. That means that nearly 60 percent of their time is spent NOT directly generating sales for your company, which is also expensive for your company in lost sales potential. I know you have heard of XYZ Company—they are in the same business as yours. Well, I met with XYZ Company nearly a year ago and they told me they also had the same problem and we were also too expensive for them. It's been nine months since I started working with them and during our last meeting they indicated to me that our new system has increased the selling time of their salespeople by 38 percent, resulting in a projected increase in sales this year of $38.8 million. By changing how they sell, their return on investment is well in excess of 16 to 1, which most companies in your business would love to achieve. That is what I am offering you here today. The reason XYZ Company decided to move forward after saying we were too expensive for them was because in the end, our system ended up costing them nothing and generating millions in additional revenues for their company. Now, what is more important for your company? Saving money by not changing or potentially generating millions of additional sales revenues at a net no-cost to you? How do you think your CFO would answer this question?"

This objection story applies to pricing, but there are many more common objections most companies will receive, so **you need to start by documenting the most common objections first and creating**

**stories for each while you move down the list.** The more stories you create, the better you will be able to address objections and successfully close a greater number of your sales.

Another form of objection commonly comes from no action at all. When customers simply "go quiet" they are still objecting you—only in a manner much more convenient to them. This is why the **"why now"** **stories should also create a strong sense of urgency in the mind of** **a buyer.** When it comes to selling, nothing sells better than scarcity because **people will demand more of what they can have less of.** What makes scarcity so powerful is that it helps create a sense of urgency that leads to action—oftentimes when a business needs sales the most. This typically includes times when seasonality can lower sales volume, when resources and inventory are too high, or when you simply need more sales to hit your sales goals. No matter what your needs, stories that emphasize scarcity can do what in many ways even price discounting cannot; namely, to get people to buy fast and buy now!

Unlike most other sales tactics that are designed around the benefits to a customer, **scarcity is the opposite due to its focus on the cost** **of inaction.**

If you are selling a service, you know that one of the most valuable resources is time since it is always limited. And since time is limited, you can use it very effectively to your advantage. Here is an example of a "why now" story using scarcity of time to your advantage: "Mr. Customer, as you know, we only hire the top designers in the industry and due to a high demand for their time, their schedules typically fill up fast. Last year we had a major project end ahead of schedule and I contacted XYZ Company to let them know that we had this rare opening they could now take advantage of. Instead of waiting for another time to open on our schedule, XYZ Company jumped at the opportunity and we got their project done in record time. Their owner even called me afterward to tell us that their business has increased dramatically due to our work and they are glad that they acted when they did.

"Well, we just recently completed another major project ahead of schedule and we now have an unexpected opening again, which is why I am coming to you first. You had previously expressed an interest in using our services and I wanted to give you the first stab at this unique opportunity before we assign it to somebody else. This is your opportunity to be like XYZ Company, and all I need is an answer from you by the end of the day so I can hold this spot for you."

## USE VISUALS TO SUPPORT YOUR STORIES

Have you ever seen a presentation when the presenter reads word for word from a PowerPoint? Nothing will put your audience and sales prospects to sleep faster. I continue to see this happen constantly and it reminds me of Sir Richard Branson's famous quote: "Communication: the thing humans forgot when we invented words."

When telling a story, always try to use visuals but ONLY use them to support your story and not the other way around. Remember, **people think in images, not in words, because visuals help create structure and meaning to words.** The problem is that far too many people over the years have become addicted to visual tools like PowerPoints in their sales meetings when what most buyers really want is a conversation instead. Use this to your advantage and **only try to use visual imagery that supports your stories with each customer, is minimal in use, and is not canned in its presentation.**

An effective visual can be anything (picture, prop, etc.) that helps to illustrate your point in a memorable way. I've seen people throw keys on tables, pull out old cell phones and old pictures—you name it—as visual aids. All of these objects help anchor your stories in a more memorable way where people will more easily remember them.

Here is an example of a visual I have used to address a pricing objection. In this case, I had a customer tell me that the price of my service was too expensive. At that point I lifted up my shoe on the table for him to see and said the following:

"Do you know what kind of shoe this is?" I asked.

"No," replied the customer, looking rather confused.

"These are $400 Bally shoes" I responded. "I would never have spent $400 on a pair of dress shoes like this if it weren't for my wife. She bought me my first pair of Bally shoes nearly five years ago and I have worn them nearly every day to work. These are the highest quality dress shoes I have ever owned. Over the years I'd bought countless pairs of cheap shoes that added together cost me far more than $400—and I never wear them! So after five years my first pair of Ballys finally wore out, and guess what I did? I bought a second pair without question because the value to me was superior to any other option. Did I want to spend another $400 on shoes? Hell no, I didn't! But what my wife taught me about value was that you either 'buy nice or buy twice,' and I never wanted to buy twice again."

As you can see, visual props can be very valuable, but there will be times when a sales prospect may request a PowerPoint or presentation instead. In these instances, you need to understand that visuals can be very powerful but NOT when they include a dense amount of text to accompany them. Most people today will literally read from PowerPoint slides and in effect turn a good opportunity for a sales conversation into a mind-numbing process. Don't do it. Keep your slides brief, remove as much text as possible, and use visuals to reinforce your story, not take the place of it. Moreover, when using visuals, make the images compelling—because your text never will be. Leave that mistake for the other salesperson to make.

When used properly, good visuals are powerful because most people think visually and not in text. Therefore, **visuals can be processed 60,000 times faster in the human brain than text** and can help give your sales prospects a point of visual focus for their thoughts as you are selling to them.[6] Because of this, it is helpful to use highly relevant and compelling visuals to help support your stories as your prospects are processing them. In many cases, the best visuals are those that match the prospect's gaps and goals, which you can uncover during initial sales conversations. For example, what if a dentist has a patient who complains that she cannot get dates because of her bad teeth? How compelling would two visuals be that help this customer see the before and after pictures of cosmetic dentistry work? Or how about a criminal defense lawyer who is meeting with a prospective client who could be convicted of a serious crime that could involve prison time, a failed marriage, and possibly losing custody of the most precious part of his life—his children? How compelling would the visualization of a new life in federal prison be versus pictures of his potential post-acquittal where he could be playing in the park with his children? What emotional impact would putting an orange jumpsuit and a pair of leg irons on a table have on that client?  The examples here are potentially endless but all are based on a visual perception of the goals and gaps for each unique customer and how your products and services can potentially help them solve their problems in the most powerful way: visually.

## DOCUMENT YOUR STORIES

As you can see, stories can become invaluable sales tools, but the final piece of this puzzle is to document your stories so you and others can use them in your sales efforts moving forward. But let's point out the obvious here first: A person can potentially create hundreds of stories, but will they remember them all and be able to use them all every day? Unless you habitually use them all over and over again each day, it is hard to program the human brain to successfully help you store and use them all. Because of this, you need to help yourself remember and recall them by documenting them.

One of the easiest ways to do this is to simply **write them down in a stories collection document (categorized by the Five Whys of Closing) and print and/or save them for easy access when you need them.** If you plan to publish and/or share stories for common use among a team of salespeople, it's a good idea to then set up a blog with secure access for your team members to easily post, manage, and retrieve your customer success stories. For more information on how to set up a sales blog, please refer to my previous book *The Successful Sales Manager: A Sales Manager's Handbook for Building Great Sales Performance,* available at dustinruge.com.

Naturally, you will not want to read your stories directly from your new stories collection document to your customer during a sales process, so it's a good idea to study and memorize them for use during a sales engagement. What should trigger each story depends on their intended use. Most stories dealing with customer introductions and customer success stories can be strategically aligned with how you run your standard sales process. Stories dealing with objections are commonly more unpredictable and can come up at any time, so make sure to trigger your stories based on the common objections received.

No matter how hard you try to "standardize" your sales process and meetings with stories, most salespeople will need to trigger all of their sales stories based on random questions and objections by your customers. Therefore, it is a good idea to role-play all of these types of scenarios with other people so your ability to trigger your stories becomes much more fluid and natural over time. Practice makes perfect.

# CHAPTER 12

# BUILD SUCCESS NETWORKS

• • •

*"A man is known by the company he keeps."*
*— Aesop*

Henry was one of the most "connected" people I have ever worked with. He would walk into a room full of businesspeople armed with something far more powerful than any product or service he could sell. He was frequently called on by contacts both near and far when somebody needed a "trusted advisor" to help answer questions within his industry, and when Henry did promote a product or service to his vast network of contacts, people listened. As a result, most vendors wanted Henry to help promote their brands because he had developed something special over the decades that their products and services alone could not do for them.

Famed author Richard Kiyosaki once said, "The richest people in the world look for and build networks. Everyone else looks for work." Henry was one of those rich people, and as a result, he never had to look for work since work was always looking for him through his vast and invaluable business network he had built over the decades. So ask yourself this simple question: If you were to leave your current job tomorrow, how many opportunities are potentially waiting for you from your own network today? If you cannot answer this question, you need to read on.

Whether you like it or not, we are living in an ever-growing and complex society. No matter how we grow both in size and technological advancements, human interaction is still largely wired the same way in our brains as well as in our behaviors that help us govern and respond to those interactions. In fact, our very own survival instincts, which have helped us to evolve, are based on our ability to "herd" with other people who share common cultures and beliefs.

This ability to more efficiently build zones of trust within groups of people is inherently no different than how our brains already wire themselves for much quicker and more efficient information processing and action. That is why we call and rely on people we know and trust for advice and direction for most everything in our lives today—it's simply less work, easier, and more efficient.

Herding also takes place in business decision-making as well. As business organizations continue to grow in size and complexity, more senior-level executives now rely on consensus from their own herd of coworkers in order to make more informed decisions.

The great part about human herds is that they always have one or more leaders—whether they choose to call themselves a leader or not. Herd leaders can always change over time and their titles alone don't always tell the whole story. For example, before I speak at conferences I always like to survey the room to see which people tend to receive the most attention from others in that room. These people are frequently herd leaders despite what their business card may tell me otherwise. Looking at LinkedIn profiles and peer-nominated awards can also provide good indications as to who may be a herd leader.

The reason initially identifying herd leaders is so important comes down to the simple use of leverage. When people like me write and publish books, we include a number of endorsements from other well-known herd leaders (authors, speakers, public figures, etc.) to help us more rapidly build credibility with others to persuade them to buy our books and, in effect, join our herd. You need to do the same thing in your work. And it all starts by following a defined process:

## IDENTIFY HERD LEADERS

In chapter 16 (Just Say "NO" to Bad Customers), we will discuss the importance of developing a targeted client profile (or avatar) for your business. This process will help you understand who your best customers are and keep you focused on finding ways to identify and sell to more of them. The next step in this process is to help identify what herds (groups, associations, memberships, etc.) your avatars belong to and then work to discover who the leaders of these herds are.

Once you have identified these herd leaders, you must find ways to get on their radar and become closely associated with them. This process can take time and require patience and persistence, but will take infinitely less time and effort than if you did the same for each member of their herd instead. Moreover, once you have a herd leader on your side, you have now developed a higher level of trust within the herd to start influencing others. This is using the power of leverage.

## USE THE POWER OF RECIPROCITY

One of the most common questions I get from people is, "How can I build influence with others?" This is especially important when approaching new herd leaders who don't know you from a hole in the wall. Well, my first advice is to stop simply following the herd and start doing things that make you stand out instead. David Ogilvy, one of the greatest advertising minds of our time, famously suggested: "Study the methods of your competitors and do the exact opposite."[1] You need to do the same thing if you want to get the attention of other herd leaders.

One of the best ways to do this is through the use of reciprocity . . . or simply giving in order to receive. **When we give to others, it is human nature for the recipient to feel an obligation to give something in return.** In your case, you may simply be looking to get their attention and time in return. In order to successfully do this, you need to start thinking outside the box and do the "opposite" of others. Here is a perfect example from my own experiences.

Thanksgiving was a uniquely special holiday in my household growing up. Every year my father would write a very thoughtful letter of reflection and thanks and send it out to the thousands of people he created connections with over the years. The responses were both unique and memorable and left an indelible impression on my life during this time of year. Now, licking and folding thousands of letters and envelopes in support of our father's efforts each fall was not something we youngsters were deeply fond of, but the life lessons we received from this process were immeasurable.

Lessons such as these are passed on through history, and my own family experiences made the holiday celebration of Thanksgiving very special to me. But these lessons have also led to greater success in business, and are something I now pass on to other salespeople.

As Americans, most of us are programmed to give around the Christmas holiday seasons. But the best way to give is when it is **personalized, unique,** and **unexpected.** Therefore, Thanksgiving is the BEST holiday season to give to others, and here is why:

Most people do not expect to receive anything from their network for Thanksgiving. In fact, most Americans are now so programmed to Black Friday discount buying the day after Thanksgiving that they forget that they don't have to wait nearly a month after the turkey goes down to start giving. Because of this, it is **UNEXPECTED** for people to receive anything from others during the holiday of Thanksgiving. Which leads us to the next benefit . . .

Since people don't expect to receive a gift of thanks during Thanksgiving, any gift you provide will be **UNIQUE, will stand out, and will be more memorable.** Remember the famous scene we discussed in chapter 10 from the movie *Christmas Vacation* when Clark Griswold brings in a gift for his boss and the reaction he received? Not only was the gift nearly identical to the other gifts on the table, but his boss's reaction was to tell him to "put in on the table with the others." This problem doesn't exist during Thanksgiving. Which leads us to the final point . . .

The best gifts should be **PERSONALIZED,** making them even more memorable. I will never forget the first year that my father's Thanksgiving letters didn't go out due to his declining health. The reactions I received from countless people truly illustrated the importance of what my father's "personalized" giving truly meant to them at that time of year. The letters he had sent out every Thanksgiving were a summary of the major events in our family over the past year along with a special touch about the importance and the true meaning of Thanksgiving. These letters were so eagerly anticipated and impactful that countless people later told me that it was "one of the things I most looked forward to receiving each Thanksgiving."

So each year, I have passed down these lessons to other salespeople by encouraging each of them to follow the same path. I instruct them to write a **PERSONALIZED** letter to their customers and hand-deliver it to their offices, along with a Thanksgiving pie, in a way that is **UNIQUE, UNEXPECTED,** and shows true appreciation. The results in sales, renewals, and customer retention alone throughout the years has been nothing short of spectacular!

The good news is you can do this at any time of the year—not just during Thanksgiving. And if you are trying to get the attention of a herd leader, make it even more personal by doing your research on them in advance. Google them, look at their LinkedIn profiles, find out what they like to do for fun, what their favorite sports team are, their family milestones and birthdays . . . anything to make it more personalized, unique, and unexpected when it comes from you.

Reciprocity can come in other ways, such as by giving your time and knowledge through public speaking. Speaking provides you with perhaps the greatest opportunity to build leverage by rapidly building credibility and trust with a large group of people in the same amount of time as an average sales call. **Since more people indicate that they fear public speaking over death itself, this is a huge competitive advantage for you if you can learn to master it.**

Public speaking, like anything else, can take time to master, so be patient and don't be afraid to speak to small groups first in order to one day get those coveted keynotes in front of your potential herd leaders—which is when your business will really start to take off.

If you are an industry-specific business professional, you should also consider joining mastermind groups with other thought leaders and professionals, which can lead to more professional referrals. For example, one of the most successful business-generating professionals I know is active in a mastermind networking group in California called ProVisors. His group meets once a month and includes a cross section of herd-leading business professionals who exchange business and contact information, ultimately leading to a high number of business referrals. He has told me time and again that this was the single most important reason for the growth of his business.

If your herd leaders tend to be movers and shakers within your local community, you should also consider giving your time to local civic groups, advisory boards for local companies, and non-profit groups as well. When joining a non-profit, stay involved and let them know that you want to one day serve on one of their committees or boards. Non-profit boards tend to be made up of powerful, wealthy, influential, and strongly connected herd leaders in their respective communities.

## DEVELOP AND LEARN FROM YOUR MENTORS

One of the great advantages in life is the ability to learn from the experiences and mistakes of others—before you need to make them yourself. One of the most effective ways to accomplish this in your career is to find a strong business mentor who can help guide you toward success. Ninety-three percent of self-made millionaires have indicated that having a mentor contributed to their success while **68 percent considered a mentor to be a "critical factor" in their success.**[2] And you should have one, too.

When seeking out a career mentor, try to find people who you can look up to, are accomplished, have a positive outlook, can be trusted, and can relate to your projected career path. Because of this, ideally you should choose a mentor who is at or near your ideal career objective, thereby helping to remove any potential conflicts of interest and ensuring they know the road ahead for you.

Once you have identified a potential mentor, make sure to tell them why you have chosen them and simply ask them if they will help mentor you. Don't worry about rejections here, for it's better to have them tell you in advance than to initially accept and then not deliver on helping you down the road. Additionally, don't be surprised if you have multiple mentors during your career as things change—that is the nature of today's business world.

When working with your new mentor, **remember that if they are successful they are also likely to be very busy people. So be respectful of their time while working with them.** Let them know exactly what you need, keep them updated on your progress, be respectful of their time, and initially keep your time requests short—they will tell you if they want more time with you or not.

## MENTOR AND TEACH OTHERS

When I work with business professionals who sometimes struggle to focus and learn, I will commonly turn the table on them by asking them to teach me and others about subjects they are dealing with. Instead of asking them to listen, process, and absorb new information, I am now asking them to help others do the same. And what a difference this can make for all involved!

**One of the greatest ways to truly learn something is by teaching it to others.** The more you teach others, the more you force yourself to learn and master a subject—which, in the end, will benefit all. Mentoring also allows you to build your own herd of followers over time. As our world becomes more digital, I have found that teaching and mentoring can scale much more quickly now, making this process even more effective. Instead of just sitting down with one person for an hour of learning, I can now record these learnings and make them available to thousands and even tens of thousands of others online for nearly the same amount of work. Talk about quickly building your own herd!

## USE LEVERAGE AND REFERRALS

One of the greatest advantages of network building is the increased amount of referral business that can come from it. There's a good reason for this as well: Familiarity builds trust and the larger your network of familiar and trusted people, the greater the likelihood you can and will receive business from them. Remember, the average consumer today is bombarded by more than 5,000 marketing messages a day; a nearly 700 percent increase over the past 40 years.[3] There is simply too much information for the human brain to constantly process each day, so we choose to rely on faster and more convenient ways to make decisions instead.

Referrals from our networks are untapped resources for most people as well. This happens because we simply don't ask for enough referrals from them! We know from studies that 91 percent of customers will provide referrals, yet only 11 percent of salespeople will ask for them.[4] If you have a network, use it! Most successful salespeople know that the larger your network, the greater the chance referral business will come from it—but only if you ask!

## CREATE A NETWORK-BUILDING STRATEGY

Now that you have hopefully learned the importance of networking and a few new ways to help you build your own network, it's time to put a strategy in place to get started. Most people want to build a strong network, but few will actually create and stick to a system to make it happen. Those few people who successfully do this are called millionaires. Recent studies have shown that **86 percent of self-made millionaires consistently dedicate their time to relationship and network building.**[5]

The most successful business networking professionals I know will **schedule around 45 minutes to an hour each day dedicated only to networking activity.** This time can include:

- Keeping up with and being active with others on LinkedIn and social media

- Making calls, sending emails, and/or writing personalized letters to others around important life events such as birthdays, health issues, marriages, deaths, business changes, etc.

- Writing thank-you/appreciation/referral letters to current and former clients—ideally on a monthly or quarterly basis.

- Scheduling future speaking/networking/mastermind/non-profit activity work.

Remember, the most important part of any activity is to initiate the new activity! So make sure it is scheduled in advance for each day and create a list of action items to run through each day you work at this. Like other activities in life, the results may not be immediate—so be patient, don't give up, and the results will follow and can eventually lead you down the path of Henry and others whose networks now work for them.

# CHAPTER 13

# MAKE YOURSELF STAND OUT

• • •

*"In order to be irreplaceable one must always be different."*
— Coco Chanel

Robert was the top salesperson at the company for three years in a row. He was the envy of the sales organization and the other salespeople like Linda tried to learn from him and even spent time selling with him to see how he did it. No matter how hard they tried, they could never seem to keep up with Robert's success. Robert, like many of the best salespeople at their respective companies, was simply an enigma to others.

One day I decided to work with Robert in the field and observe what he was doing. Like most successful salespeople, Robert had a high activity level, was very smart with his time, and knew who to meet with and why. Robert had a plan for success. But there was something else about Robert that made him stand out—his customers loved working with him. Our first two meetings together were with his key customers, who had increased their buying with us over the past few years to what were now some of the highest levels in the company.

When the meetings started, you could tell that the relationships developed between Robert and the customers were strong and that there was an extremely high level of trust between them. Knowing that I was organizationally at a level above Robert, the customers acted toward me in a way that practically advocated for Robert as if he were one of their people working for me. I remember a couple of comments made to me by these customers stating that, "If it weren't for Robert, I wouldn't be with your company" and "Every time one of your competitors calls us, and they call us a lot, I simply tell them to talk to Robert."

After a number of customer meetings, Robert and I had lunch and time to debrief. I was then able to learn a little more about Robert in a more casual setting.

"Robert, tell me a little bit about your career." I said. "I saw from your LinkedIn profile that you've been with us for nearly four years now."

"Wow—has it already been four years?" Robert responded with a surprised look on his face. "It's amazing how time has flown since I first came here."

"So how did you first learn about our company?" I asked.

"It was the same thing that led me to every other company I've have worked for, I guess," replied Robert. "David and I used to work together at a previous company, and when he came to work here he let me know about the opportunity when it opened. It seemed like a great opportunity, so I jumped at it."

"Why was the opportunity here so much better than at your previous company?" I asked. "Did you not do well there?"

"No, I've been the top salesperson at each of my last three companies," Robert quickly replied. "What I liked the most here was that the compensation plan allows me to earn more money than at my previous companies. I don't want this to come across the wrong way, but I know I can eventually become the top salesperson at any company I work for, so I want to work for a company that rewards my performance instead of capping my income potential."

"Looking at your LinkedIn profile, I noticed that one of your previous employers has been struggling for years and another is no longer in business," I said to Robert. "Did you leave because you had to sell inferior products at those companies, and was that holding you back at the time?"

"That's just it, Dustin," replied Robert. "I have worked for companies that had the best and worst products in their respective industries and it never really affected my sales numbers. Two of those companies were in the exact same industry selling competing products and I sold as much of the bad products for one of them as I did the good products for the other."

One of the key observations I made early on in my sales career is that the best salespeople will typically strive to be the **best salespeople no matter where they work and what they sell.** I would constantly see great salespeople move from companies with superior products and services to companies with vastly inferior offerings and vice versa, and the results were almost always the same. People like Robert could successfully sell nearly anything under any circumstances. So how did they do it? And what about all those excuses you may hear from salespeople about how if only their products or services were better they could be the top salesperson as well? As we saw with Robert, all of this ultimately starts with the salesperson and a clear understanding that **HOW YOU SELL is more important than what you sell.**

People buy from people, especially people they like. Likability comes from a number of factors including similarity, compliments made, and your willingness to be helpful and cooperative. Likability also comes from a willingness to genuinely care for the well-being and outcomes of your customers when working with them.

For most salespeople today, it's important to understand that you represent your brand and **in many cases you become your own brand while selling others.** As our economy continues to mature, we are faced with increasing levels of competition and commoditization of our products and services. When commoditization takes place, the greatest differentiator often comes down to price. That is, unless you can add more personal brand value to the sales process than your competitors. As a result, the salesperson representing their products and/or services is likely to have a greater influence on the customer's perception of your value than the services you provide.

Studies of consumers now confirm this by indicating that **35 percent of the value they receive comes from the person selling the products or services alone.**[1] This applies to brand loyalty as well. Your company can build the most powerful brand in your industry that everybody may know, **but the brand alone does not know your customers— only you do.** Because of this, **your customers will typically be much more loyal to you than the brand you represent.**

So in order for you to better sell your products and/or services, you need to be able to sell yourselves first. You can do this by first understanding that YOU are also a unique brand in and of yourself, and you must develop ways to better build credibility and trust in the eyes of your customers. You also need to take steps to better develop the perceived value that you provide in your relationships with your clients. This is commonly done when you are able to do the following better than your competition:

- **Provide reasons to buy from you beyond just the products and services that you offer.** This often means providing additional value-added experiences and services to help support the sale. It is important to remember that in sales, **you have to give in order to receive.**

- **Ask intelligent questions** of your customers in a way that allows you to understand their issues and needs better than your competitors.

- ALWAYS make your customers **feel like they are the most important people** to you and your business when they are taking their time to deal with you. Every customer interaction should be designed to exceed your customers' expectations and make them feel as important as possible.

- **Connect personally before you sell professionally.** Salespeople often talk about being "in control" of the sales process, but they often fail at knowing when the appropriate time to take control is. There is an old saying: "People don't care what you know until they know that you care." People have an inherent need to feel important, and the best way to make them feel important is to start out by personally connecting with them. Look for areas of similarity and common interests, and offer compliments. When you begin any sales meeting with a prospect, always try to make a personal connection before you jump into business. If they have a problem and/or need, acknowledge it, understand it, empathize with it, and connect with it. If I find a customer is upset, I always let them talk it out first and then reply with a simple response: "I don't blame you one bit for feeling the way that you do. If I were in your shoes, I would likely feel the same way." I ONLY start to control a sales process after a connection is first made. This requires getting any negative emotions and/or fears out of the way, and I will often let people talk themselves out before I ultimately steer them to where I want to go.

In summary, most professionals cannot count on their services alone to be their differentiator in today's business climate. Moreover, when you develop a sales process for your business you will find that the execution of that process is what truly sets you apart from others, and the people who make that execution happen have the key to success.

## THE FIVE-YEAR-EXPERT PLAN

There is a prevailing belief among many people that those who master an art or a profession were simply born with that gift. If you've ever heard anybody proclaim that a person is "a natural born salesperson" you know what I mean. But recent studies are beginning to shed more light on this subject, and what was once a common belief is now becoming more of a myth.

In Malcom Gladwell's groundbreaking book *Outliers: The Story of Success,* Gladwell builds on a study by Anders Ericsson that suggests that **people are not born to greatness but rather become great through hard work and persistence . . . and a lot of it at that.** The assertion is that the human brain has limitations, and only by committing one's self to a long period of learning and practice—no less than 10,000 hours—can one truly become great at their craft.[2]

Many of these more recognizable "great" people include Mozart, Robert Oppenheimer, Bill Gates, the members of the Beatles, Wernher

Von Braun, and countless others. In the case of the Beatles, Ericsson's research revealed that since the band played in Hamburg, Germany, more than 1,200 times between 1960–1964, adding up to around 10,000 hours of performing, it led them to uniquely master their performances moving forward. The rest, of course, is history.

This mastery can be found in nearly all facets of our society. Former president Ronald Reagan was commonly referred to as "The Great Communicator" and often credited his ability to master his communication skills to hosting GE Theater and speaking at more than 135 plants over eight years prior to going into politics. These examples are all around us every day and most came from simple hard work and dedication.

**If you chose sales as a profession, you need to start training yourself as a sales professional.** Unlike other professions, most people are never formally educated and trained in sales until after they start selling. Doctors, lawyers, accountants, and most other major professions require years of learning and/or certification to start practicing, and for good reason—as Ericsson discovered, it takes the average person around 10,000 hours to truly master a chosen discipline.[3] And if the maximum amount of hours the average person will work is 2,350 hours per year, it could take you at least four to five years to hit this level of mastery. So how do you get started?

**The first step is to set a goal and write it down.** If you are in sales and you want to become the best salesperson possible, you have to make this commitment to yourself. The next step is to find something you are truly passionate about and never settle for selling anything less as a long-term objective. Some people will learn how to sell in larger, more structured sales environments—many of which are designed to train and weed out young salespeople early in their careers. Others will sell for smaller organizations that have little or no sales structures whatsoever.

Whichever path you chose, it is always a good idea to experience a number of different environments early in your career, for the experiences and learning you will receive will become invaluable. For example, when I first decided to pursue sales as a profession, I was working for a very large corporation at their headquarters during that time. I signed up for nearly all the sales training courses they provided and began working in very complex sales cycles involving dozens of people all working in coordination.

Following this highly structured environment, I decided to swing the pendulum by working for a small technology start-up, where I had to handle everything from responding to RFPs to writing proposals to post-sales support. Had I not seen and experienced each of these vastly different sales environments, I would have been much slower in developing my career. But no matter where I worked, one thing always remained consistent: educational reading!

The world is full of information based on the lives and experience of others and the good news for you is that most of this information is captured and available to you both online and in books. There are all types of books, both fiction and non-fiction, but **millionaires tend to read to acquire and maintain knowledge.** In fact, studies have shown that 88 percent of self-made millionaires devote at least thirty minutes or more to educational reading—and so should you.[4]

In chapter 7, I have included my own recommended reading list for salespeople to start this journey. Certainly there are many other great books and more to follow, but to me, these are the foundational books I recommend to other salespeople to get started in this process. But there are additional ways you can learn from others as well.

As discussed in the previous chapter on how to build success networks, having and learning from mentors can be critical to your success and learning as well. Much like an educational book, mentoring allows you to learn from the experiences and knowledge of others and further set you ahead in your career.

## HELP OTHERS PROPERLY INTRODUCE YOU

I will never forget an important lesson I learned early on in my speaking career. It was perhaps one of the largest groups of people I had ever spoken in front of at that point in my career. Nearly a thousand people, many of whom were learning about me for the first time, paid attention as the MC introduced me to the audience prior to me speaking. Looking down at his notes, his introduction went something like this: "The next speaker has written a number of books for sales managers and frequently speaks to groups like ours about how to get the most out of our salespeople. So I am happy to introduce Dustin Ruge." (He pronounced my last name as "RUG.")

One of the great things about having a unique last name like "Ruge" is that most people don't know how to properly pronounce it (ROO-gee). This can be entertaining at times but can work against you as well in certain settings. But it wasn't just my name he got wrong. In fact, the whole introduction was so wrong in so many ways that I felt like I was placed into a very deep hole that I now needed to dig myself out of—all thanks to a simple but deadly introduction to others. I swore to myself that this would not happen to me again. It is a lesson you should take note of as well.

Introductions to others take place in all types of settings—not just when you speak. In fact, if you're in sales, you are likely to get introduced to others daily in many different ways including in person, by email, on the phone, when you speak, etc. When this happens, we often take for granted that the person introducing us will make a proper introduction. But as you saw from my previous speaking appearance, this is frequently not the case. And that is where you need to step in and help.

If you are in sales, you have a number of things you need to remember and use often—and your opening that others will use to introduce you should be one of them. Some of these situations, like an introduction before a speech, can be prepared for and provided in advance while other situations, such as a quick phone call on your behalf, typically cannot. Either way, you need to be prepared because **the opening citation you receive from others can be just as important as the content you provide afterward.** Why? Because people tend to rely heavily on the credibility provided by others—the more credible the source, the more credibly you will be received by others. But even if the source providing your introduction is credible, **what that source does or doesn't say about you can be just as important.** So here are a few ways you can make sure that your introductory message used by others is as strong as possible.

First, **make sure your digital footprint is strong and consistent.** This means that when somebody Googles your name on their own, the top search results they see should say about you what you want people to convey to others on your behalf. Web properties at the top of these digital footprints can typically include your own website, professional profile pages, your LinkedIn profile, social media pages, etc. Google your name to find out what shows the highest for you—typically the top five to ten search results—and take control of them now.

Second, **write a few copies of your introduction** in an easy-to-read, larger-text document, and have them ready to provide to any MC, host, or promoter prior to any meeting or speaking engagement. Don't just rely on what you tell them, for most will typically get it wrong. This is why having a written copy with you at all work times is critical to helping make the most of your introductions.

Third, **create a high-quality two-to-three minute introduction video about yourself** for others to view on websites, from your email signature, and prior to speaking if the format will allow for it. Ideally your video should include strong testimonials from other, similar customers, and clearly and strongly answer the question "Why you?" in the minds of everybody who watches it. People love watching videos and this is your chance to really nail it home and make yourself stand out from others . . . especially since you are likely to be the only salesperson with such a strong and distinguishing introduction.

Finally, make sure that your introductions are easy for others to find. In addition to always bringing printed copies with you, make sure they are also optimized within your digital footprint and linked to from your email signatures. If you have a video intro, you can also create an image thumbnail for your email signature and link it to a copy on your website, Facebook page, YouTube page, and/or LinkedIn page for easy access and viewing.

## QUICKLY BUILD TRUST AND RESPECT

There is an old saying in business that you never get a second chance to make a good first impression. Well, scientists have recently indicated that this **first impression is typically made in less than three seconds and can become the difference between somebody liking you and wanting to do business with you and not.**[5] There are a number of factors people will initially judge you by but the two most critical are whether they trust and respect you.[6]

Of these two factors, the most important is trust—and most people will judge your trustworthiness in less than a second. How? Oftentimes by your facial expressions alone. In a recent study, university students were shown pictures of actors' faces, but some were able to view them for only a fraction of a second. They were then asked to rate each picture by attractiveness, likability, competence, trustworthiness, and aggressiveness.

Two very interesting findings came from the study: First, the strongest correlation of results was around **trustworthiness,** and second, the students who were given unlimited time to view and rate the pictures produced largely the same results, although they become slightly more negative over time.[7]

Judging people by their facial features and expressions is nothing new. Studies on facial features and trust have shown that people **view "happy" people with higher levels of honesty, reliability, and trust.**[8] Taking this a step further, the facial structures we tend to subconsciously assign greater levels of trust to just so happen to mirror a "happy-looking" face.[9]

To illustrate this point in a less scientific manner, when you first meet a dog up close, notice how they react to a happy face versus an angry face. I have done this with dogs countless times to see just how quickly they will react to my facial expressions, and it works almost every time.

So how can you as a salesperson apply this information to help you improve your own sales? Here are a few tips:

- **Don't meet with new clients and sales prospects while you are in a bad mood.** Bad moods internally will often be reflected in how you act externally, and it will show—especially on your face. If you are having a really bad day and you have important sales meetings ahead, simply reschedule them for a time when your bad mood goes away.

- **Train yourself to smile more around other people.** If actors can train themselves to do this on stage, you can train yourself to do this in real life. Always start your greeting with anybody new with a smile, eye contact, and a firm handshake. Make everybody you meet with feel like they are the most important person to you at that time.

One of the most amazing parts about a smile is how it can affect your attitude, confidence, and sales results. When a salesperson initially starts out a sales month with a strong sell, they will commonly end the month with very high sales results—all because of their attitude and the confidence that they then carry into each subsequent sales meeting. So make your attitude shine and watch your sales grow; it all starts with a smile.

Respect (or credibility and competence) is the second most important factor people will initially judge you by, yet many salespeople continue to lead with respect over trust despite people continuing to judge you in the opposite order. Again, people don't care what you know if they don't know that you care. Once trust is established, here are a few simple ways you can help quickly build higher levels of credibility and competence during a sales process:

- **Become an expert in your chosen profession.** Everybody loves credentials, prominent awards, and recognition. Why? Because it conveys a unique level of competency, credibility, and trust with your prospective customers, which can help lead to increased sales, revenues, and higher customer conversions. By becoming and expert you can then ask intelligent questions about your sales prospects' needs and problems, which will help you gain credibility with the **prospect.** Finally, you can also be seen as more of an expert by publishing articles, blog posts, books, and speaking on specific topics and to trade groups.

- Get in the habit of asking for **referral business.** Referrals are commonly your best prospective new customers because they are typically introduced by a citation that invokes a higher level of trust and credibility before the sales process even begins.

- Create greater awareness and familiarity for yourself and your brands BEFORE your sales process begins—which is one of the best ways you can increase your initial sales conversion rates. Let's face it: We all get bombarded every day with increasing levels of advertising. **The average person now receives around 5,000 marketing messages a day; a nearly 700 percent increase over the past 40 years.** As a result, nurtured leads convert better and **make 47 percent larger purchases than non-nurtured leads.**[10] Remember, not everybody is ready to buy when you want to sell to them. Therefore, good nurturing by email, mailers, public speaking, ads, etc., should include useful information to your sales prospects that also conveys your level of skill and expertise, as well as results your services have provided to others.

- Build greater consistency and consensus in your sales. Many people buy based on the exposure and the buying actions of others. If they see others buying your products and services, they become more curious and see you with a higher level of credibility and trust as a result. People by their very nature like to stay in their comfort zones and tend to buy in a similar manner. This is the reason people will frequent the same stores and restaurants to buy the same clothes and order the same food; they know what to expect each time they buy. As a sales professional, your customers will have the same expectations of you and your offerings. Therefore, if they refer you to one of their family, friends, or acquaintances, they are putting their own credibility on the line with the expectation that you will deliver the same level of service and results to the referral that you provided them.

- Ditch the canned presentations and start with a conversation. Recent studies have indicated that 88 percent of executive buyers now want a conversation and not a presentation.[11] Because of this simple fact, you need to design your initial sales interactions as a conversation—let the other guys blow it by selling like a robot.

- Arm yourself with many happy customers. **Most salespeople will tell you that the best tool you can arm them with is happy customers.** Why? Because happy customers create the strongest credibility possible; namely, proof of the value you are trying to sell to others. And that is the name of the game in sales: rapidly developing credibility and trust with your buyers during the buying process by simply invoking the value you have provided to similar others.

These are simply some of many ways you can quickly build more credibility, trust, and respect both during and before the sales process begins. For more information on this topic, please refer to my previous book *The Top 20%—Why 80% of Small Businesses Fail at Sales & Marketing and How You Can Succeed,* available at dustinruge.com.

## PROJECT SUCCESS

*"If you are not a brand, you're a commodity."*

Have you ever met somebody that simply "appeared" successful? Perhaps it was the way they dressed, their posture, their confidence, their composure, or the way they talked. Or maybe it was all of these things and more. Harry was one of those people. When Harry walked into any room, he commanded attention. He was always dressed to the nines. He always greeted others with a smile on his face and he exuded confidence in anything he did—even when he was wrong. Harry was also VERY successful and you could see it.

Harry didn't start out this way. He grew up in a rough part of Brooklyn, New York, and had to fight for everything he had early on in his life. Nothing was ever handed to him and he was the first in his family to ever graduate from college. Put simply, Harry knew what he wanted early on in life and knew what he had to do in order to achieve it.

I learned a number of life lessons from Harry that have stuck with me throughout my career. Many of them are simple in nature but brilliant in their outcomes. One of the first lessons was about how I dressed in my work. The second time Harry and I met was during a lunch meeting at a major conference. The conversation was not one of my typical lunch meetings.

"Dustin, you and I both sell to powerful people in New York City," said Harry. "What do you notice about them when you first meet with them?"

"Well, most of them have really nice offices in the best parts of the city," I replied while thinking out loud.

"What else do you notice when you approach them to shake their hands?" asked Harry. "How are they dressed?"

"Most of them wear really nice suits—typically Armani or better," I replied.

"Right!" exclaimed Harry while leaning forward to look me in the eye. "They look like they are successful. And how did that make you feel when you first met them?"

"I little intimidated at first," I replied. "Most of the people I know who dress like that are some of the most successful and intelligent people I know."

"Now, take a look at how you are dressed right now," said Harry while pointing at my jacket. "Don't be offended by this question, but where did you get that suit, shirt, tie, and shoes you are wearing?"

"I bought this suit on sale at Men's Wearhouse near my office in Midtown and the rest came from various other stores—typically while on sale," I replied with a little bit of hesitation. Nobody likes to look inferior in front of others, but I wasn't going to lie to protect my ego.

"On Friday I want you to meet me for lunch again," said Harry. "Only afterward, I'm going to introduce you to my tailor, Sal, who works right around the corner."

Now, Harry must have known what was initially going through my mind. I was a younger business professional at the time working in New York City and many of these people I was selling to had a number of years on me; they had a lot more time to earn, live, and afford to dress the way they did. Although I wanted to trust Harry's advice, I was also fighting back my own skepticism.

"Harry, I'm sure he's great," I said. "Hell, you always look great every time I see you! But I'm not sure I can afford to buy tailored business clothes from Sal right now," I said.

Harry sat up straight in his chair, pulled down his jacket to remove any creases, and with a serious look replied, "Dustin, you are one of the smartest people I have ever met and you have a unique gift. But these people are not going to help you become more successful until you look the part first. **They are not going to give you their money until you look like somebody who knows what to do with it.** You have made a significant investment in your education and now it's time to make another investment in your presentation. Both are investments in your success."

Harry was right—it was time to up my game. That Friday we met with Sal, he took my measurements, and I started on my way to a whole new wardrobe. I explained my situation and Sal understood. Not only was he a great tailor, but he was also a great salesperson.

"Dustin, how many of your current suits, shirts, shoes, and ties in your closet do you wear on a regular basis?" asked Sal.

After pondering his personal inquisition for a moment, I embarrassingly replied, "Probably only twenty percent."

"But you are wearing a nice pair of shoes," said Sal while looking down at my feet. "It looks like you wear those more than twenty percent of the time, no?"

"My wife bought these for me a year ago and I never would have spent that kind of money on shoes had she not bought them for me," I replied. "But I wear them almost every day and I love them."

"Dustin, in my world, **you either buy nice or you buy twice,"** said Sal. "In your case, what you spend with me will cost you far less than what you have spent filling your closet with useless clothing. The difference is you will wear my clothes and, more important, you will be more successful because you will look and feel more successful."

One of the trends currently taking place in today's workforce largely goes against what Sal correctly taught me that day. Year after year a growing number of larger organizations are moving to a "casual" dress code in their offices. As a result, there is a very good chance you will be selling for organizations with people wearing jeans and short-sleeve shirts supporting you.

Now, I don't want to delve too deep into this subject, but I do strongly believe that **how one dresses impacts how they feel and how they project themselves to others—whether it be in person, on the phone, by email, etc.** I have even proven this in practice by taking inside salespeople—those who only interact with people over the phone—and increasing their performance by simply upgrading their dress code at work.

In summary, how you dress says a lot about you both to yourself and others. Much like writing down a goal, how you dress sends a signal to yourself and others about where you want to be in your career. In sales, you have a very short time to make a good first impression and unless you can project a high level of success in your appearance, you are putting yourself at an immediate disadvantage. And this all starts with how you present yourself to others.

The good news is that your sales competition is heading in the wrong direction here and you now have a chance to use this to your own advantage by becoming a more unique brand in and of yourself. Remember: If you are not a brand, you're a commodity, and selling as a commodity always comes down to one thing: price. Your brand and the brand you represent should represent unique value—for a valuable brand is what sets you and your business apart from others.

# — CHAPTER 14 —

# THE EVOLUTION OF SALES METHODOLOGIES

• • •

*"Learning never exhausts the mind."*
*— Leonardo da Vinci*

I was recently asked by a new college graduate if his business degree was enough to succeed in today's business world or if he should continue on to graduate school to get his MBA. Jimmy seemed like a pretty bright kid to me but like so many people just finishing school, he was also looking for "the perfect job" to get started in and wanted to know if his degree was strong enough to get him there.

I looked Jimmy straight in the eye and asked, "Jimmy, what did you learn in college?"

"Well, I received a degree in business administration," he replied with a rather curious look on his face.

"I meant what did you learn, not what your degree says," I responded.

Jimmy just stood there, still looking confused. I could tell he was struggling to say something and after a brief and rather awkward pause he replied, "I don't know what you mean."

I smiled at him and said, "Jimmy, when I hire people, I want people who are capable of learning and learning fast. Most good companies today are in need of employees who are capable of critical thinking. The only thing a college degree or MBA really tells me is that you are capable of learning in a structured environment. Most people mistakenly graduate with their credentials, throw their caps in the air, and then sell their textbooks to fund a celebratory drinking spree, thinking that they've now learned enough to become successful in business. My business school books are still on my shelves decades later along with hundreds of newer business and sales books I've read along the way. Do you know why I still keep them there?"

"No," replied Jimmy.

"Because they're a reminder to me that learning never stops and you never know enough," I said. "Your degree in whatever caliber it comes will simply be your starting point in your lifelong learning process. Therefore, my suggestion for you is to buy a large bookshelf, save a few of your favorite business school books, and start your own collection. Every day you'll look at that empty shelf and it will remind you that just like in life, you have only begun to learn. And if you want to make it in sales, well, welcome to the other fifteen million Americans who sell without a degree in sales. You might have a degree, but your education has only just begun."

## EARNING YOUR DEGREE IN SALES

**No other profession in the United States produces more workers without a degree and without credentials than sales.** Some of the greatest salespeople of our time even lacked a formal college education, but that didn't mean they were incapable of learning how to sell. There are two primary ways you can learn how to sell: You can learn by making mistakes and reinventing the wheel or you can learn from the mistakes and experiences of others and gain an immediate advantage over those who don't. The choice is yours.

Since there is no real degree in sales, when you graduate from college most employers have to take it upon themselves to train you to sell. **This should be one of your primary considerations when looking for your first sales job: What will your employer offer to help train and make you a better sales professional?** When I started in sales, I signed up for literally any and all sales training classes offered by my employer. When I decided that I wanted to be in sales, I knew I was already behind every other seasoned salesperson at my company simply because most salespeople learn through experience and I had practically none at that time. This is where many companies fail, and you need to take it upon yourself to succeed.

Far too many companies "initially train" their salespeople and then let them go. They continue to repeat this process over and over again until they ultimately realize one of two things: either they cannot afford the constant turnover in sales personnel anymore or they are going out of business. Both are real outcomes, yet history always seems to repeat for those who fail to learn from it.

Over the course of weeks, months, quarters, and years, we see constant changes in markets, companies, buying behaviors, technologies, competitors, pricing, and sales strategies. Therefore what we learn at inception is often outdated, and the longer the duration between sales trainings, the worse this can get. Salespeople want to succeed and achieve, but they cannot do it all on their own; they have the same need for improvement as someone in any other profession.

Since salespeople by nature develop sales habits through practice, **you have to constantly challenge yourself to learn and become more productive.** Because of this, learning should take place in phases and be constant in your career. In the perfect world, learning in doses would take place on a weekly and monthly basis. The key is to make sure what you learn is useful, helpful, relevant, valuable, actionable, and, just as important, is provided by a credible source.

Learning is also supported by personal goal setting. For example, I make it a personal goal to read at least two books every month. We also know from studies that 88 percent of self-made millionaires will educationally read for 30 minutes or more each day.[1] Whatever your company provides to supplement your learning should also be pursued, but don't rely on them alone or you will fall behind in your progress to becoming a top sales professional.

# WHAT SALESPEOPLE HAVE
# LEARNED OVER THE YEARS

Up until the twentieth century, sales was largely based on a simple barter system, which later evolved using currency exchanges. Back in those days, people learned sales through experience. Around the turn of the century came the Industrial Revolution, leading to larger companies, growing metropolitan areas of "untrusted neighbors," and products that were quickly becoming more commoditized and harder to distinguish. At this point, many organizations started to see the need for more standardized and scalable sales processes.

The first such standardization came from sales and advertising pioneer E. St. Elmo Lewis with the creation of the "AIDA" framework, which stood for Attention, Interest, Desire, and Action. This largely linear process was one of the first major attempts to adapt how we sell to how people buy. After AIDA, the first real breakthrough came in 1936 with the release of Dale Carnegie's book *How to Win Friends & Influence People,* which quickly became all the rage in the sales profession and the foundation for nearly all sales methodologies moving forward. This book is so foundational to business success that it is still the first book I recommend all people who go into business read.

What made Carnegie's book so remarkable was his focus on how to better deal and work with other people. With the rapid growth of ever-larger and more complex business organizations, the timing of this book couldn't have been any better. Anybody who has worked within the "corporate world" knows full well that the more people you have to work with, the more complex and political organizations tend to become.

Following the release of Carnegie's book, a number of sales methodologies emerged but none of them really caught fire until 1968 when Xerox provided the foundation of modern sales methodologies through the creation of "Needs Satisfaction Selling." First developed by Don Hammalian at Xerox, the basic premise behind Needs Satisfaction Selling was to ask buyers what was important to them and then introduce benefits of products and services that helped to satisfy those needs. This was in contrast to more traditional sales training, which commonly taught salespeople to more rigidly control the sales process and stressed being able to "sell anything to anybody."

Like most innovations, Xerox's new sales methodology came out of necessity. At the time, Xerox was in the process of losing their patent to dry photocopying and was concerned about the growing levels of sales competition that would result from it. The result was an unprecedented $10 million investment by Xerox to help keep their salespeople ahead of their competition and product commoditization by helping them to change "how" they sell. In short, this methodology was based on the belief that people love to buy but hate being sold; therefore, by better informing the customer, they will make better buying decisions.

The next major evolution in sales came in the 1970s with the release of *Strategic Selling* by Robert Miller and Stephen Heiman—both former IBM salespeople. This book was more strategic and tactical in nature and focused on how to handle more complex sales and how to better identify key decision makers in the sales process, including the all-important economic buyer (the one who writes the check). Additional works by these same authors are still in use today when dealing with very complex sales.

In the 1980s came a number of key advancements in sales methodologies, leading to the release of the books *Solution Selling* by Michael T. Bosworth and *SPIN Selling* by Neil Rackham. *Solution Selling* taught salespeople to identify and sell to a customer's pains—with the solution (or sell) being the resolution of the customer's pain. The essential premise being "no pain, no gain (or sale)." This concept was useful assuming the customer had a recognizable pain. For example, we know that when people buy, 70 percent will buy to solve a problem while only 30 percent will buy to gain something—so the concept certainly speaks to a larger portion of the buyers, but clearly not all of it.[2]

*SPIN Selling* (SPIN being an acronym for Situation, Problem, Implication, and Need-Payoff) was focused on sales tactics that helped turn reluctant buyers into willing buyers. *SPIN Selling* expanded on the older Xerox sales models by getting the customer more involved with the sales process, asking detailed questions, getting to know their needs and expectations, and challenging their conventional ways of problem solving. In short, this more "consultative" approach to selling teaches how to ask detailed and intelligent questions of the customers and encourages salespeople to act more as a consultant than a traditional salesperson.

The most recent major evolution to these sales methodologies comes from *The Challenger Sale,* written by Matthew Dixon and Brent Adamson of the Corporate Executive Board (CEB). What makes this new sales methodology so unique is that it actually downplays relationship building and instead teaches salespeople to "challenge" the customer's conventional way of thinking and take greater control of the sale by selling through the education of the customer.

*The Challenger Sale* also classifies salespeople into five different categories, claiming that that "challenger" salesperson, who represents only around 27 percent of the salesforce, has certain key traits, including their ability to view the world differently, their ability to truly understand the customer's business, their love to debate, and their ability to "push" the customer when needed.[3]

Beyond these more standard methodologies, the advent of the Internet, social media, and mobile technologies are also changing how we buy and sell. Consumers are in far more control of sales information than ever before and more often than not will be able to thoroughly research a product, service, and company long before a traditional sales process will ever begin. Because of this, you need to better understand where exactly your customer is relative to the "Five Whys of Closing" before your sales engagement begins with them.

Looking at the evolution of all of these sales methodologies, it is amazing how some of them have in many ways come full circle while others are simply evolutions of previous thinking. There are many more methodologies beyond this list that have been developed—but my goal was to focus on the most notable of these since many of the others are simply variations of the same.

The important point to remember is that all of these methodologies have contributed in some way to making salespeople better through the learnings and experiences of others. Some methodologies are also a better fit to certain sales and industries than others. So which is the best one? It really depends, and the more research that is conducted, the more we are bound to learn moving forward.

## LOOKING FOR ANSWERS WITHIN

As we continue to learn and expand our sales methodologies it's also important to note the recent research into why they are working for certain salespeople and not for others by looking inward at the human brain and habits. Many recent works— including *What Great Salespeople Do,* published in 2012 by Michael Bosworth and Ben Zoldan, and *Outliers* by Malcolm Gladwell—speak to the recent developments in neuroscience and the time commitments needed to reach expert status in our lives—a good deal of which we touch on in detail within this book. In many respects, these new books provide greater insight into how we are genetically wired to buy, sell, learn, communicate, and become highly skilled in our professional lives beyond simply following sales methodologies.

Recent developments in neuroscience have also led to the more recent publishing of books such as *The Power of Habit* by Charles Duhigg in 2012 and *Change Your Habits, Change Your Life* by Tom Corley in 2016, which take a much deeper look at human nature and how much impact daily habits and taking control of them truly have on many of our successes and failures in life.

Prior to these recent works, most companies continued to rely on the previously discussed sales methodologies deployed at the company level to address sales performance issues. But as we are now learning, sales methodologies alone do not explain nor do they solve the growing discrepancy in sales performance and results between the top 13 percent of producers and everybody else. This is why a focus on systems both at the business and personal levels is necessary to fully address this issue, and why further sales methodologies are likely to follow.

# CHAPTER 15

# BUILDING A SUCCESSFUL SALES PROCESS

• • •

*"Systems permit ordinary people to produce*
*extraordinary results—predictably."*
*— Michael E. Gerber*

"I never had to learn a detailed sales system until I started working here," said Linda with a slightly overwhelmed look on her face.

"So what kind of sales systems did you have exposure to prior to joining this company?" I asked.

"Well, most of the places I worked at before simply let the sales-people figure it out on their own," replied Linda. "I mean, we still had to report our weekly sales activity in an email to our manager, but beyond that we pretty much had to ask others or figure it out on our own."

"So how was that experience compared to what you're dealing with today? I asked.

"There seems like a lot of new things I have to do now and it can be a bit overwhelming at times," replied Linda. "I work pretty well on my own and I don't know why I need to follow all these steps and complete all this reporting to be successful."

"So let's take a step back for a moment, prior to when you started working here," I said. "You mentioned that you had to largely figure it out on your own back then. How long did it take you to really figure it out, and when you did, how did you document and share that information with others?"

"Well, I guess we all initially struggled for a while," replied Linda.

"Some, like me, eventually figured it out, while many simply didn't make it and left. Once we figured it out, most of us had a pretty good idea what to do from that point forward."

"And where was that information then saved?" I asked.

"Right here," replied Linda while pointing at her head with a smile on her face.

Linda's experience is certainly not unique. Only 65 percent of businesses today indicate that they have a defined sales process.[1] This basically means that **roughly one-third of all businesses are winging it when it comes to sales—the smaller the organization, the more likely you are to see this.** Great businesses of any size are run by systems, and those systems are run by people; not the other way around. Sales is no exception.

There are many benefits to having a good sales process. The most successful businesses are those that are run by systems and processes that make people interchangeable and not the other way around. When it comes to sales, most businesses will always have some level of turnover in staff, will end up hiring good and bad performers, and will see varying results. The goal, then, should be to create and constantly refine your sales process, for a good sales process can:

- Help reduce your costs of sales and increase your sales efficiency
- Help standardize your reporting and performance metrics
- Help simplify sales management and allow you to make better decisions
- Help increase productivity and share best practices for the entire sales organization
- Help improve the performance and onboarding of new hires
- Help increase sales efficiency through detailed opportunity analysis
- Help increase sales-forecasting efforts for the business

No matter what business you are in, people who buy tend to go through the same psychological buying patterns, which a standard sales process should be created to match. You can modify this process to best fit your own business, but as a basis to start from, below are the major elements of a standard sales process. Since a good sales process will follow a set of sales stages (or steps), here are the primary ones to start with.

## PROSPECTING

First comes **prospecting.** Prospecting is the most important part of any sales process, for without sales prospects, there is nobody to sell to. You have to be able to identify your target market, know how you are going to most effectively reach them, and create and follow a defined and disciplined prospecting plan. The goal of this stage is to try to produce as many high-quality leads as possible with the least amount of time and cost to support your sales objectives.

## APPOINTMENT SETTING/CONVERSION

Second is sales **lead conversion/appointment setting.** Now that you are generating sales leads, how are you converting them into a sales opportunity (typically defined by a sales call or appointment)? This is a critical part of your sales process that many businesses and sales professionals fail at doing well since the timing, processes, resources, and systems in which you can convert leads into sales opportunities can typically have the most dramatic impact on your Cost per Lead (CPL) and your overall Customer Acquisition Costs (CAC).

## CUSTOMER QUALIFICATION

Third is the **customer-qualification process.** Qualification of your sales prospects typically takes place during a meeting and/or over the phone. But with the advent of the Internet, more people now have access to far more information about their sales prospects prior to a sales meeting than ever before—so use this to your advantage.

During this stage you are trying to uncover key information such as **who the primary decision maker is** and how purchasing decisions like these are typically made within their organization. What are their **goals** that define where they want to be over a defined period of time, such as three to five years from now? What are their **gaps** (problems or needs) that you can sell to that will make the difference between where they are today and where they want to be (their goals)? **Can they afford your service/s,** and do they really need/want it? **Are they able to change** to your product/service if the product/service is currently being provided by somebody else, and if not, when will they be able to potentially change? **Does your product/service really provide a higher alternative level of value** than what they currently have without it?

The main point to keep in mind here is that poorly run businesses and the people who sell for them typically do not know what a qualified customer is, how to properly qualify a customer, and do not follow a repeatable customer-qualification process. As a result, many salespeople think they have a qualified customer when they really do not. The fact that up to 60 percent of all sales end in a non-decision should tell you all you need to know about what is really qualified and what is not in today's business world. **We also know from studies that most sales are made or lost within the first three minutes,**[2] which typically involves the time you spend initially qualifying a customer.

In order to address these key breakdowns, it is always a good idea to create a simple customer-qualification form/process that you and other salespeople can easily follow to make sure that the questions asked and the order they are asked in are as standardized and repeatable as possible. You can download examples of these at dustinruge.com.

Once you start adding more salespeople to this process, you can spend more time refining the process instead of just relying on each person to figure it out on their own. This is the quickest way to help build a scalable sales operation.

## PRESENTATION/POSITIONING

The fourth step is your sales **presentation/positioning.** Once you have determined a potential customer has a need/want that you can sell to, how do you go about positioning your products/services to address that need and, more important, how can you articulate that value to that specific customer? This is where things can get dicey for many salespeople—they need to learn how to present their products/services while also keeping the client engaged in the process. In most cases, salespeople will break into a PowerPoint or some type of canned presentation, which is the surest way to start losing your prospect. Studies have shown that **88 percent of executive buyers want a conversation and not a presentation,** which is where you can now set yourself apart from your competition.[2] By having a conversation instead of a sales presentation, you can then repeat back the key elements you have documented in your client-qualification form and strategically seed that information into your service pitch to make it the most relevant and impactful to your prospect.

Don't be afraid to use visuals in your presentations, but ONLY use them to support your conversation and not the other way around. Remember, **people think in images, not words, because visuals help to create structure and meaning to words.** The problem is that far too many people over the years have become addicted to visual sales tools like PowerPoints in their sales presentations when what most buyers really want is a conversation instead. Use this to your advantage and try to only use visual imagery in a way that supports your conversation with each client, is minimal in use, and is not just canned in its presentation.

Finally, remember that **people love to buy but hate to be sold.** So don't sell them anything—help them to buy. The only way you can most effectively do this is by giving them options—whether you end up being one of them or not. The point is that people are always weighing their options and asking themselves "Compared to what?" Because of this, **your biggest competition is always "doing nothing," which is why 60 percent of sales end in no decision.**[2] To control the sales process, help define the options for your prospects (what they have to gain and what they have to lose by choosing each) and let them decide for themselves. Just make sure not to provide them with too many options; two to three are typically sufficient, because you can start to confuse them with any more than that.

## DEALING WITH SALES OBJECTIONS AND DELAYS

The fifth step is **overcoming any objections and delays.** "I have to think about it." "It's too expensive." "Let me get back to you." Ever heard these objections before? Of course; we all have—people use them every day and they will use them with you, too. When people get to a buying decision, they buy based on two factors: **greed and fear.** Both of these words are based in emotion, and what ultimately compels people to buy is an emotional reaction relative to their own "why." It's up to you to discover it and help compel them to want to buy.

The first thing to remember about objections and delays is that you may have not yet lost the deal; the prospect is simply throwing you a lifeline. The question now is: How do you react to it? **Most delays are the result of one or more concerns** that the prospect has that you have not yet addressed. Unless you can address them, in their eyes the value of what you are providing is not worth the value of the money it will cost them to buy it.

The second point to remember is that prospective customers are **not looking for the cheapest option but rather the highest value.** Ask yourself: Do you buy the cheapest clothes you can find? Do you drive the cheapest car or live in the cheapest house? Of course you don't. Why? Because you find a higher level of value in the clothing, cars, and housing you choose for yourself. How high is too high in cost? Each person has to ask that question of themselves, and a good qualification process will help you uncover it for your sales prospects as well, even if your prospect may not yet know it themselves.

**Most price objections end up having nothing to do with pricing and everything to do with something else**—most of which you should have been able to help identify through a good customer-qualification process. If you find yourself running into a lot of pricing objections, go back to your qualification questions and see what you were missing before you got to this point, and see if this is happening with other prospects as well. The more commonality in objections you are seeing, the more this becomes a process issue you can help address at the sales-process level. **In most cases, there is either a lack of need/ want, a lack of trust, a lack of value, and/or a lack of urgency on behalf of the customer that you have not uncovered up until this point.**

The best thing you can do when you receive delays and objections is what your sales prospects will least expect: **Stop selling and start listening.** Most people who sell will react to objections emotionally and start trying to sell them again. Don't do this—reverse psychology is what wins here for most. Here are the steps that will help you better address objections:

1. **Listen intently** to the objection of the prospect, show empathy, nod along with them, and **repeat their objections back to them.** This sense of empathy can send a strong signal to the person you are selling to that you understand and care about their concerns.

2. After you have repeated their objection back to them, **explore deeper into the issue/s to find out what the true reason is for the objection.** Remember, the reason you commonly hear the same sales objections over and over again is because they are the easiest for people to remember and use in a non-offensive way. A typical response at this point might be: "I understand. Can I ask you a question? What are your concerns about this decision right now? What is it that you may be uncomfortable with so I can make sure you have everything you need to make an informed decision when you are ready?"

3. Once all objections have been discovered, **address each objection** and then ask if you have addressed their concerns to their satisfaction.

4. If all concerns have been successfully addressed, briefly recap their goals, gaps, and the benefits provided by your solution and ask

them, "Would it now make sense to move forward?" If not, go back again to addressing their needs until THEY indicate they are comfortable moving forward. If they are ready, you can start your closing process. If they still want to delay, simply ask them, "When would you like to start seeing (repeat back their goals here)?" If they see no sense of urgency in moving forward now, they clearly don't see the value exchange—which goes back to your sales process.

## THE CLOSE

Sixth is the **close.** Now the fun part: You are ready to close the deal. But are you really ready? How do you know? The best way to gauge whether a sale is actually ready to close is by asking trial-closing questions. One of the biggest challenges in selling is not in being able to qualify the prospect but rather getting them to close when they are ready. We know from studies that **50 percent of all sales leads are qualified but not yet ready to buy.**[3] Why? Because many times we are trying to close business on our time instead of our customers'. This is where sales-people frequently make mistakes and become desperate, and then start to discount and provide other concessions to close what is not yet ready to be closed. This also means that whatever concessions you have now provided to that customer will be expected by that customer when they are ready to close—even at some later time.

Trial-closing questions are a great alternative to simply asking for the close because they are typically non-threatening and highly informative. For example, some of my favorite trial-closing questions include: "Is there anything that might prevent you from moving forward with this decision (*today, this week, etc.*)?" "Have you decided when you would like to start seeing (*repeat goals back to them*)?" "Are you still planning on moving forward with (*repeat back goals*) this (*week, month, etc.*)?" "Are we still in good shape to get started some-time this (*day, week, month, etc.*)?" "If you were in my shoes, is there anything you would be doing differently?" And my all-time favorite is to start a trial-closing question with agreement to action by asking, "Would it now make sense to . . . ?"

Once you have successfully used a trial-closing question, you should be ready for the close. So what are you waiting for? Around **78 percent of salespeople will hesitate when it comes time to ask for the sale, and two-thirds will end a sales meeting without asking at all.**[4] Why would so many salespeople waste so much time and so many resources to prospect, generate leads, and conduct sales meetings and then never ask for the sale?

There is only one final goal in your sales process and that is to close business. How else are you going to attract new clients, pay your bills, and reach your goals if you do not ask for it first? Remember, **if you never ask for what you want in business, the answer will always be "no."** So don't be afraid to ask, and build a habit of always asking. Based on the sales process we have discussed, you should already know and have articulated to the prospect the value of their action and inaction and provided them with two to three buying options to consider. Once they have the options in front of them, it is time for THEM to buy. And here is how you can help.

The first close option you have is the **"hard close."** In this case, ALWAYS be confident when asking for a close because your body language and tone of voice will tell them more about your confidence than anything else you can say to them at this point. When you ask for any commitment and/or signature, lean forward, confidently look the sales prospect in the eye, and make sure to repeat back the incremental value they will receive for that price. If they need to sign, hand them your pen while they look down at the sales agreement. If you want them to sign electronically, hand them your device and do the same. Once that is done, **shut up** and continue to confidently look them in the eye and wait for them to talk next. If they talk first, they will typically buy. If you talk first, you could lose the sale. Remember the old saying: **"He who speaks first loses."** So fight the temptation to say anything and confidently shut up and wait for the buying signal, which should always come first from the buyer and NOT FROM YOU.

The second type of closing option is the **"soft close."** A soft close is a more subtle closing tactic that **implies to the prospect that the sale is already expected and therefore next steps are now asked of them.** In many ways a soft close resembles a trial-close question, only the next step is what typically takes place after the sale is made. For example, if you have to set up a post-sales meeting or appointment with a client, a soft close would be to ask them, "Looking at your calendar, how does next Tuesday look for our first meeting and/or appointment?" Or, "My calendar typically fills up quickly, so when is the first available day and time that we can get started?"

Notice how subtle and non-threatening a soft close can be to a customer. Oftentimes when I have a salesperson I am working with who has a low closing ratio, I will get them in the habit of using soft-closing techniques, which can dramatically increase their close rates as well as their habit of and confidence in wanting to ask for a close.

If either closing technique is met with a refusal to move forward, it will usually mean there is an objection that was not adequately addressed in your sales process prior to the close. In those cases, go back in the process and address the objections again as you did before. The trick is to **NOT GIVE UP.** Just because somebody is giving you a "no" now doesn't mean you have lost the sale, yet that it is exactly what most salespeople assume. Consider the following:[4]

- 44 percent of salespeople give up after the first "no"
- 22 percent of salespeople give up after the second "no"
- 14 percent of salespeople give up after the third "no"
- 12 percent of salespeople give up after the fourth "no"

Looking at these numbers, we can see that all but 8 percent of salespeople will give up on a sale before they reach the fifth attempt to close it. We also know that, on average, **60 percent of customers will say "no" four times before they say "yes" to a sale.**[4] So as you can see, discipline in sales is the name of the game, and closing is not only a game of action but persistence and eventually getting to "yes."

## ASK FOR REFERRALS

Seventh is asking for **referral business.** Referrals are commonly your best prospective customers because they are typically introduced by a citation that invokes a higher level of trust and credibility before the sales process ever begins. Despite this fact, many people struggle with effective prospecting when it comes to asking for referrals. We know that in business today, 91 percent of customers will provide referrals, yet only 11 percent of salespeople will ask for them.[2] This "failure to ask" primarily comes from the following three reasons:

1.  Most salespeople DO NOT *consistently* ask for referrals
2.  Most salespeople DO NOT **ask for referrals from the *right customers***
3.  Most salespeople DO NOT **ask for referrals in the *right situations and settings***

The most effective way to deal with these failures in asking for referrals is to change your habits and discipline surrounding your potential referrals. Here are a few effective ways to do this:

- First you need to understand that there are only three types of customers you will ever sell to: Promoters, Buyers, and Demoters. Of these three types of customers, you need to focus as much time and energy helping your **Promoters,** because if you consistently help them, they are the ONLY customers who will help you in return. Most salespeople stop asking for referrals because they fail to understand that **Promoters are your best potential source for referrals that lead to the fewest rejections.** So start by identifying and nurturing your relationships with your Promoters.

- Many referral attempts fail because of a simple issue of location. If you ask customers for referrals in their home or work settings, you are competing with their time and daily habitual distractions. If you ask over the phone, you are dealing with the same competing interests. But when you **take a customer out to**

**breakfast or lunch,** you have sixty minutes of their time dedicated to you—typically without common distractions. Change the setting and you change the focus—resulting in more and better referrals.

- In sales, nearly every agreement involves some form of negotiation. When prospective customers want concessions from you, you should ALWAYS know what concessions you can ask for in return. A great salesperson will always keep a list of concessions (including asking for referrals) in their mind. And never forget that if you never ask for something, the answer is always "no." So **the next time a customer asks for a discount, ask for five referrals in return**—quid pro quo.

- If you are in sales, stop acting like you are not. Your customers know you are in sales and therefore they should not be surprised if you ask them for sales-related help. Always end every customer engagement with a simple question: **"Mr./Mrs. (*customer name*), would you happen to know of any people in your network who could benefit from my products and/or services?"** You may not always get the answer you want the first time you ask, but if they expect the same question again from you during future engagements, watch what happens.

## GENERATE REPEAT AND BOOMERANG BUSINESS

Eighth is generating **repeat and boomerang business.** Many of the best sales professionals will have a high level of repeat business. Recurring customer sales are critical to any business due to the high cost of new customer acquisition, which can run seven times the cost of acquiring business from your existing customers. Moreover, the **return on investment (ROI) of client retention activities is typically ten times higher than for new-client marketing.** Therefore, it is important that you not only deliver a higher value of service to your current customers, but that you stay in frequent contact with them as well. A general rule of thumb in your marketing plan should be to follow the Rule of 12 and make sure that you reach out and "touch" your existing customers at least once a month by email, newsletter, social media, etc.

You will also have sales that never close when you wanted them to close. Many of these prospects will typically go quiet or continue to say "no" to your attempts to close them. The longer you are selling for a business, the larger this pool of previous sales prospects can become. So what happens when most salespeople do not initially close an opportunity? They move on and leave an opportunity that may still be closable in the future. The challenge with most sales opportunity management systems today is that once a lead moves to a sales opportunity and fails to close within a defined time frame (typically defined by the business on a daily, weekly, monthly, or quarterly basis), the opportunity is then "moved out" and often discarded. And when an opportunity is discarded, so too is the opportunity to close it again when the customer is ready to buy on their time—not yours.

For most salespeople, the ugly truth is that not all people and opportunities are ready and willing to close **when YOU want them to close.** Because many of our sales processes start by initiating contact with a potential prospect, we know that around 50 percent of qualified leads are NOT YET ready to close. The surest sign of this happening is when a prospect seems to "go quiet" during the sales process. Just because you may need to make a sale and hit your sales objectives this week, month, or quarter DOES NOT mean that the customer is working under the same time frame. If 50 percent of sales leads are qualified but are not yet ready to buy, even the best salespeople cannot get them all to buy on their schedule alone. In the best cases, only half of those 50 percent can be persuaded based on timing alone while the other half cannot. The bottom line here is that **just because the "timing" of the opportunity is off doesn't mean that the opportunity is off.**

When an opportunity is not ready to close, it should be nurtured until it is. **Businesses that nurture sales leads on a consistent basis typically produce 50 percent more sales-ready leads and at a one-third lower cost.**[3] The problem is that the majority of sales organizations today have no lead-nurturing programs in place. In the case of sales opportunities that fail to close in a forecasted time frame, many of these leads may still in fact be qualified. Therefore, the Rule of 12 should be applied to each. The Rule of 12 comes from marketing research that tells us that you need to be in front of a sales prospect at least 12 times a year for them to "actively" remember you when they are ready to buy. The problem with the Rule of 12 for some salespeople comes from when they initially follow up on sales leads with constant and repeated closing attempts that end up turning many people off. Again, this is the result of trying to close an opportunity before it is ready to close. There is a better way.

**When a sale and prospect goes quiet, all of these opportunities should be immediately moved into a boomerang (or nurtured) sales process.** A boomerang sale is nothing more than an opportunity that is delayed for whatever reason but comes back later to close when the buyer is ready to buy. Since many salespeople cannot predict exactly when this time frame may be, they need to move their sales process from a close to a nurturing stage for each of these opportunities. In short, when the client says "no" and/or goes quiet after multiple closing attempts, they are typically not yet closable and should move into a boomerang communications stage of your sales process. In order to do this, the following are four easy steps any salesperson can follow:

1. When a forecasted opportunity fails to close after multiple attempts, the opportunity classification should be moved to a **boomerang sales opportunity** in your sales pipeline.

2. Boomerang sales pipeline opportunities should be *treated differently* than other opportunities because you have already engaged the prospect in your sales process and therefore what you are trying to accomplish with them (a delayed close) is inherently different than what you are trying to accomplish with the remainder of your sales pipeline (starting a new sales process). This requires that you classify these boomerang opportunities differently in whatever you are using to manage your opportunities today—CRM, spreadsheets,

databases, etc. This new classification will now allow you to quickly filter, manage, and/or export this contact data for use.

3. Once you segment your boomerang clients out, you need to stay in front of them on a consistent basis in a way that strikes a balance between too much contact and too little. The two most cost-effective ways to do this are through social media and email. Email still has a very high level of reach since most people have email and frequently access most/all of their emails daily. Social media is more segmented—meaning that your postings will display chronologically based on user access. Therefore, the organic reach of social media can be very low based on the chances of your post being seen at the time of their system access. Because of this, a general rule of thumb for boomerang clients is **once a month by email** and **once a day by social media.** Some social media experts will tell you that three times a day is the maximum reach on social media, but for nurturing leads, this can be both excessive and unrealistic for most salespeople. With the recent advancements in social media advertising, including website and activity tracking, you can do this much more effectively than in the past. So should you only use email over social media? No. Email may have three times the number of users as social media, but not all of them can be reached by one medium alone, so it is best to use both if possible for maximum reach.

4. Finally, your messages to "stay in front" of your boomerang prospects should be **informative and helpful to the prospect—*NOT salesy!*** The goal of these emails is to keep your name actively in front of these sales prospects and give them additional reasons to WANT to buy from you. In this case, by providing them with useful and helpful information that they can use, you can better establish yourself as a credible and trusted advisor in the eyes of the prospects.

By following these four simple steps, you can convert more of your boomerang opportunities into an active and convertible sales funnel. Based on my own experience, when executed on correctly, I have seen a **20 percent sales bump** on average for those businesses that have adopted this model of better handling boomerang sales.

## CREATE A SALES MANUAL ONLINE

The final step is to document these processes for easy access, training, and use by yourself and others. Prior to the proliferation of blogging technology, I would always create a sales manual for others to follow. One of the most famous sales manuals ever created was written by David Ogilvy in 1935. Back then, David was a star salesperson of the Standard AGA Cooker (a home kitchen oven/stove) in England. He was so successful at selling that his company asked him to create a sales manual for others to follow—which many people even today consider to be one of the finest sales manuals even written.

Today, I have found that sales manuals are more effective when they are published online for easier access and use—commonly using a blog platform such a Blogger or WordPress. One of the added benefits of a blog platform is the ability to allow users to easily edit, curate, and add to this information online without having to make constant edits, reprinting, and redistribution over time.

# CHAPTER 16

# JUST SAY "NO" TO BAD CUSTOMERS

• • •

*"Choose your customers. Fire the ones that*
*hurt your ability to deliver the right story to the others."*
*— Seth Godin*

A few years back I worked with Michael, who was a well-known bankruptcy trustee lawyer on the East Coast. During our regular meetings, Michael would frequently ask what I could do to help generate even more business for his practice. When I asked him how much business he currently received, his answer was always "more than I can handle." Yet he still wanted more. This story may sound a bit perplexing to many people, but Michael ran one of the most successful legal businesses I've ever worked with, and his secret was his command of the word "no."

Michael's story helps illustrate the true power of supply and demand in any form of business—including sales. When I asked Michael why he wanted even more clients despite the fact that he was already overloaded, his response was that he learned something most attorneys have not—namely, how to say "no" to any potential client that comes his way. This ability to freely refuse any new customer allowed Michael to better pick and choose the most desirable and valuable customers for him. The more potential customers he had to choose from, the greater the opportunity for success without the guilt and wasted time. As a result, he was able to increase his billing rates and income and free up his time to do more of what he loves the most: fishing.

The first step in successfully using this process for yourself is to **set a goal of generating more business prospects than you can handle.** So how much business is too much business? This is the question that most businesspeople will ask themselves, and it is the wrong question based on the wrong goals. The goal of every customer engagement should be to maximize the value exchange for both parties, which means being too busy is not always being the right kind of busy.

Most salespeople today only prospect, network, market, and advertise to their desired level of potential customers and then stop. Because of this, most salespeople always fear a potential future drop in business, which increases their levels of paranoia and obligation. This commonly leads to lower sales volume, lower average order values, and the retention of undesirable customers. All of this can be solved with one simple solution: Always set your goals to constantly increase your volume of new potential customers. When you do this, you will have more potential customers to choose from, leading to better customers, higher average order values, and higher sales.

Bottom line: For sales to grow you need to be able to attract more and better new customers who will help promote that value to others. In order to do this, you first need to start by determining who exactly these ideal customers are.

## CREATE A TARGET CLIENT PROFILE (AVATAR)

One of many responsibilities you have as a salesperson is to make sure you and your resources are as productive as possible. One of the most effective ways to start in this direction is to make sure you are selling your products and services to the right customers. This may sound counterintuitive to some people, but not every customer is the right customer. Yes, they may all initially be able to buy your products and services and therefore increase your sales, but at what cost to your business does this happen?

**We know from studies that it costs, on average, seven times more to acquire a new customer than to retain a current one.**[1] Once a customer is acquired and the initial sale is made, what value or lack thereof does that customer pose to your business and future sales? And how do you know in the end that you sold to the right customer?

One of the most effective ways to answer these questions is by creating, marketing to, and selling to a specific Target Client Profile (or avatar). A Target Client Profile is nothing more than a picture and description of the ideal customer for your business. If you already have an established base of customers, start by profiling who among them you consider to be your best customers and find the commonalities among them. If you are new to a business, start by painting a picture of who you expect will receive the highest level of customer value from your products and services and how they can help you spread that value to others.

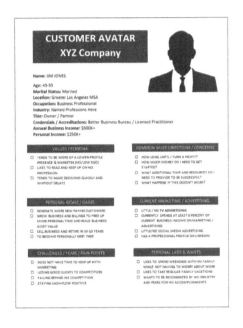

When creating your Target Client Profile, define your ideal customers' demographics and characteristics in detail. This may include details such as where they live and work; their age, gender, and occupation; their company sizes and industries; how much they typically spend on similar services; who else successfully sells to them and how; and why and how they make purchasing decisions today.

Secondly, you need to define their **common problems** and what they are **trying to gain.** Remember, people make purchasing decisions based primarily on these two factors, so you must understand what these are before selling your services to them. If what you sell is not considered a higher-value product/service and fails to provide a compelling enough reason for your Target Client Profile to want to make a change, it will not matter how good it is if nobody ends up buying it.

Finally, you need to publish your Target Client Profile and make sure that you clearly understand it. You should also make sure that anybody who works with and helps to support you is also aware of this profile, for it will have impacts on and help define all aspects of your sales growth moving forward. This is especially true when it comes to marketing.

Far too many businesses today continue to bifurcate the roles of sales and marketing. One of the best ways to help bridge this gap is to make sure your marketing resources have a clear picture of your ideal client avatar and, more important, align their marketing resources and activities strictly around these people. Remember: You cannot sell to people who cannot and will not buy, so keeping all of your sales and marketing resources and activities focused on your avatars is critical to your sales success.

## FOCUS ON CUSTOMERS WHO WILL HELP YOU SELL

*"Get closer than ever to your customers. So close that you*
*tell them what they need before they realize it themselves."*
—Steve Jobs

Most salespeople sell to customers without being able to properly segment them. When you create your Target Client Profile (avatar), you help to define who your ideal customer is. The problem, however, is that nearly all salespeople will continue to sell and retain customers outside of their Target Client Profile. In fact, this may have been going on for years before you ever defined your own customer segmentation process.

**As a salesperson, you must be able to properly segment your customer base so you can maximize your sales efficiency for you and**

**any people supporting you.** Absent this, you will never be able to fully address your customer and sales problems.

For example, we've all had what most would consider to be "problem" customers. These people can be a drain on you, your people, your business, and your resources. Over a customer's life cycle, these people are sold to at a higher overall "cost" of doing business with them. On the opposite side of the spectrum, you will have customers who fit your Target Client Profile (avatar) and you will always want more of them. The problem is that most people don't understand the value of customer segmentation and will end up wasting far too much of their time with problem customers at the expense of their Target Client Profile customers.

To help address this issue, you should start by segmenting all of your customers into three simple category designations: Promoters, Buyers, and Demoters.

## PROMOTERS

A number of years ago I attended a Salesforce.com customer event in New York City. At the time, Salesforce.com was not yet widely known or adopted in the CRM community; they were an up-and-coming company. I was considering Salesforce.com as an integration partner with a software company I owned so I thought I would attend the event and see what their customers were saying.

The roughly one-hour meeting started off with the Salesforce.com representatives asking a group of a couple hundred customers in the audience what they thought of their CRM system. What followed for the next thirty minutes left me speechless. One customer after another stood up and had nothing but glowing reviews for Salesforce.com and their CRM service. A few customers even said that Salesforce.com was charging their customers TOO LITTLE based on the value they were receiving. Now, how many businesses have had this happen to them? I was sold. This was either the greatest show ever produced outside of Hollywood or I had just sat through one of the best and most effective customer-supported sales events in my lifetime.

What this customer event illustrated, among many things, was the power of customer promoters. **"Promoters" are those customers who, if you help them, will help you in return.** You will typically know who these customers are when you first sell to them: **If they are good to sell to, they are good to have as customers.** In the Salesforce.com customer meeting the room was filled with Promoters, and what they were doing—intentionally or not—is exactly what any business wants their customers to do: help them more effectively sell their products and services to others.

In most industries, Promoters will range anywhere from 10–25 percent of your total potential customer base. Their percentages may be relatively small, **but the multiplier effects they can have on your business can be astronomical.** As a salesperson, you need to understand and be able to explain to other people who work with you that these are the customers they should be giving the majority of their time and effort to. The returns to your business can be enormous, but only if you know who these people are and how best to manage them.

## BUYERS

The largest segment of potential customers—around 50 percent for most businesses—are people who simply buy your products or services and do nothing else. They don't try to help you sell to others and they typically don't complain, either. What makes this segment of customers unique is that they are typically the largest buying block in any one market, and they are not considered early adopters.

Early adopters typically represent up to 15 percent of a typical market and they like to buy early and often. Early adopters are the people who buy the newest and greatest TV so they can be one of the first to own it. They also buy the next new iPhone model to be released when what they already use will typically meet their needs.

**Buyers are different from early adopters because they more often purchase to solve a problem** instead of trying to gain something. Because of this, **they are more inherently skeptical than other buyers and oftentimes require proof and successful citations from others**

**before they will buy.** This is where Promoters come in and can become so valuable to you.

Promoters will help you sell to Buyers. By helping Promoters, they in turn will help you by providing valuable success stories, references, referrals, etc., that are needed to successfully sell to Buyers. The problem is that most salespeople don't understand this and instead spend far too much time with the wrong customers—called Demoters.

## DEMOTERS

When most professionals talk about their "bad" customers, they are usually referring to a "Demoter." A Demoter is a customer you CANNOT make happy. You can make them money and even make them successful, but you cannot, no matter how hard you try, make them happy. Demoters may sometimes fit within your Target Client Profile (avatar) but by their very nature **lack loyalty, are undesirable customers, and are a drain on your sales and business.**

Much like with Promoters, Demoters are typically a smaller segment of a potential customer base, ranging anywhere from 20–30 percent in most industries. **You will typically know who these people are when you sell to them because they are hard to sell to.** This should be your first indication of a potential Demoter. If they are hard to sell to, they are hard to manage as a customer.

**Demoters are also takers by nature and therefore will do NOTHING to help you and your business grow your sales.** If you help them, they will commonly not help you in return. The most common reward people receive by helping Demoters is keeping them quiet and not complaining. This is the heart of the problem with Demoters: They love to complain and we waste far too much of our valuable time trying to make them happy. In the end, we cannot make them happy and all the time wasted was time that would have been better spent helping our Promoters instead.

In summary, it is just as important for you as a salesperson to know what will help make you successful as WHAT WILL NOT. You are going to receive both bad customers as well as good ones, and that will NEVER change—it is the nature of sales, marketing, and advertising. So embrace this reality, create and refine a solid system to help manage and scale it, and learn when to say "no." This is exactly what nearly all top salespeople are able to do and what you should be able to as well.

— CHAPTER 17 —

# PLAN FOR JOB CHANGES— STARTING NOW!

• • •

*"Change is inevitable. Change for the better is a full-time job."*
— *Adlai Stevenson*

Brett loved flashy cars, nice watches, and his extravagant lifestyle. Brett was also one of the best salespeople I have ever worked with and his sales results were truly remarkable. In three years, this young generation X-er was on top of the world and was selling more every year than nearly the bottom half of the salesforce combined! Brett was exactly what every salesperson in the company wanted to be and he wasn't shy about flaunting his success for all to see.

But as successful as Brett was in his job, he was failing in building a career that could ultimately take him to the next level. You see, Brett's performance and résumé were stellar but he was also stuck in his job— a product of his own personal financial and career mismanagement. As with most great sales jobs today, all glory is fleeting, and what was once Brett's great cash cow ultimately became his albatross.

What Brett should have realized is that the average tenure for a sales professional today is only around two years.[1] Now, many people would argue that this number is the result of so many poor salespeople that will wash out, but that doesn't tell the whole story. Gone are the days of our grandparents, who worked in one job throughout their careers, earned their pensions, and then retired—all with the same company. Today, the velocity of change and innovation in our economy is so rapid that many of the businesses we may work for today may never even survive the length of our own careers—so accept it now and embrace it. We now know that fully 55 percent of businesses will fail in five years and of the original Fortune 500 companies listed in 1955, 87 percent are now gone from that list.[2] Change is now everywhere—including in your career.

But job changes aren't just the result of company actions. Recent studies have indicated that 68 percent of salespeople plan to look for a new job over the next year.[3] The top five factors listed for why they would consider leaving their jobs include:

- Salary and compensation (74 percent)

- Career and growth opportunities (65 percent)

- Company culture (48 percent)

- Relationship with manager (46 percent)

- Senior leadership (38 percent)

Now, before you jump to the conclusion that most people want to leave to make more money, consider that 71 percent indicated that they would work for LESS MONEY to work for a company with a great culture, and 78 percent would accept LESS MONEY to sell something that is particularly more compelling to them. In short, **although money is important to most salespeople, where they work and what they sell can be of equal or even greater value.**

Now, for three years, Brett was working for a company that many considered to have a good culture and great products—all the things many salespeople look for in a job. The problem was that Brett's company was acquired shortly thereafter and all of that changed. The first casualty was the lucrative compensation plan that had originally attracted highly driven salespeople like Brett to come sell for the company to begin with. The new management thought the salespeople were being paid too much, so a new marginalized compensation plan went into place.

The second casualty was the company culture with the purge of the previous senior leadership, which was replaced by "yes men" with practically no leadership qualities. These new managers were people who had simply "risen" to the top by merely surviving decades of attrition and were ultimately the last people standing. Finally came the new sales leadership, who knew practically nothing about the culture that had made Brett's previous sales organization great, and who decided that rigid micromanagement was now in order.

Within the first six months of these new changes, most of the top salespeople had left the company—nearly all except Brett. Instead, he had two things working against him. First, Brett was fiercely loyal and continued to hold out hope that the good old days would one day return to his company if he just waited a little bit longer. Brett would always tell people that he loved his company even though everything he had previously loved about his company had already changed. All except for Brett's blind devotion.

Second and most important, Brett spent every dollar he ever earned by creating a lifestyle that was simply not sustainable. When the money increasingly came in for the first three years, it was easy for Brett to think that the good times would always roll on, so he spent money like a drunken sailor in anticipation of a better future ahead that ultimately never came. Now when recruiters would call, Brett couldn't afford to take a financial risk by working for smaller companies that couldn't provide benefits. Brett also had a number of great offers to work for other companies in other cities but simply couldn't afford to move his family and take the risk. He was even recruited to become a sales manager at his company but couldn't afford the pay cut. In the end, Brett was stuck, and what was once a great job had now led him down a path of a failing career—all because he had never prepared for change.

## THE ONLY CERTAINTY IN YOUR CAREER IS CHANGE

In a free market economy there is no greater threat to your economic liberty than debt—and Americans now have a lot it! According to recent studies, nearly half (47 percent) of Americans now live paycheck to paycheck.[4] And don't think this is only a problem for people at or near the poverty level. We also know that around 25 percent of these people make more than $100,000 per year, like Brett did.[5]

To make matters worse, most Americans today, especially those of the younger generation, truly suck at saving money. Fully 56 percent of Americans studied now indicate that they have less than $1,000 in their savings and checking accounts combined.[6] And the younger the generation, the worse this problem is becoming. Throw on top of all this the nearly $1.44 trillion in student debt (or around 9 percent of the US economy) we are also shackling our younger generation with.

What people like Brett should have known is that if you want to be highly successful in sales, you need to avoid this financial trap—starting now! When you create a lifestyle and career that requires you to live paycheck to paycheck, you are creating a dependence that leads you to servitude, and servitude is the enemy of career mobility and freedom.

So does this situation apply to you now? Let me ask you this question: What prevents you from walking out of your current job right now? This should be an easy question to ask since nearly 68 percent of salespeople indicate they are already considering this option. Some might answer that they won't leave because they love their jobs. But what if I were to tell you that I have a much better job waiting for you? Do you think you would still leave? Or what happens when your "loved" job involuntarily changes like it did for Brett? If you are struggling with any of these questions, you need to start asking yourself why—now!

## SAVING BUYS MOBILITY AND FREEDOM

> *"If you don't find a way to make money*
> *while you sleep, you will work until you die."*
> —Warren Buffett

If you want to become a millionaire in sales, you need to start doing what the millionaires do with their money. First, you need to set the proper expectations and understand that 88 percent of self-made millionaires became wealthy after the age of 50.[7] Most of their wealth did not come overnight but through decades of disciplined saving and investing. So let's start by discussing savings.

**You need to save at least 15–20 percent of your income starting as early as possible.** The earlier you start saving, the faster your money will start earning more money and start working for you. For example, if you saved $1,000 a month for 30 years while earning 6 percent interest, your total investment of $360,000 in payments will result in a total of $1 million dollars in savings in 30 years. In order to help automate this process, have your bank set up a separate savings account where a percentage of your earned income (10–20 percent) is automatically removed from your checking account into this special savings account each month for you.

The second consideration should be how you save. Many investment experts will tell you to save your money for retirement due to the tax advantages of deferred taxation. The problem is this money, if dedicated for retirement, typically becomes untouchable (or illiquid) for most people throughout their careers and can incur a very high penalty for early withdrawal. That is why you need to start saving in two ways: The first is for your retirement and the second is for your mobility. There are also hybrid options such as saving in Roth IRAs, so make sure to consult with an investment advisor to learn more about all of your investment options.

When you save for mobility, you are basically saving money that is relatively liquid (or easy to access without penalty) so you **have a pool of money to allow you to more freely make job and career changes when YOU want to make them.** How much you save as mobility savings is up to you, but many people will suggest anywhere from **6–12 months of your normal living expenses is a good position to start with.** Based on this goal, I always suggest initially increasing your savings percentages until this initial amount is created and maintained— at which point you can reduce further saving percentages if needed.

Your next consideration is investing your savings. Again, with the exception of Roth IRAs, most retirement savings accounts will limit how, where, and when you can invest your money. As for your mobility savings, the world is your oyster and you can invest wherever you please. This takes us to yet **another financial trait of self-made millionaires: fully 67 percent of them have more than one stream of income, with around three being the most common number.**[8]

By developing multiple sources of income during your earning years, you can better diversify your income streams and better weather changes when they arise. Many of these streams of income can come from investments that pay returns (or dividends) over time, such as investments in real estate, the stock market, annuities, part ownership in a side business, services, intellectual property royalties, etc. The most popular of these options tends to be ownership in real estate rentals. But keep in mind that buying these properties can also help make you relatively immobile if you get a job offer that requires you to transfer a long distance from where your real estate is owned. So if you plan to stay put, this has always been a popular investment option.

No matter where you choose to live, you will also have another piece of real estate online that will always be with you and is something you will need to invest in as well.

## BUILD OUT YOUR DIGITAL FOOTPRINT

**Most people today, whether they know it or not, have a personal online (or digital) footprint,** and it is growing exponentially every day. Just Google your name and see what comes up on the first page for your own search results. In some instances you have direct control over parts of your digital footprint through tools like your websites, blogs, and the social media that you control. However, the largest part of your footprint, the one typically controlled by third-party sources, is the fastest-growing component of your footprint and the one consumers are placing a greater amount of trust in than ever before. This is why proactive personal online brand management is becoming so important.

Branding is a critical consideration in hiring as well. Recent studies have shown that **65 percent of hiring managers now use social media sites to research sales candidates before hiring,** 49 percent said they have not hired someone based on their social media presence, and 41 percent have indicated that they are less likely to hire people they cannot find information about online.[9] Since a growing portion of your digital footprint involves social media, it is a good idea to make sure that what you want to be seen is seen and vice versa BEFORE you start looking for a new job.

A good example of the power of branding comes from the story of McDonald's. One of the questions I frequently ask groups I speak to is, "Who sells the best hamburger in the world?" Names of all types of burger chains and even home chefs will fly around, but the one name always missing just so happens to be the name of the company that has sold more hamburgers than any other company in the world: McDonald's. Why? Simple: You may hate the product, but you understand the brand. You know what the name McDonald's promises to provide you each and every time at any of their locations throughout the world. Why? Because you and your children—along with nearly every person in the United States—are familiar with the name. What this also illustrates is that **the most important element of branding is consistency**—something you need to focus on heavily with your own personal brand as well.

Creating an effective personal brand-management strategy involves a process of taking control of your brand footprint and staying in control of it over time. The last thing you want a potential employer to find when researching your digital footprint is an inconsistent message—especially as it pertains to your career. For example, I remember researching a job candidate for a very high-profile sales position that required a good deal of social involvement when selling to this particular type of customer. The candidate's LinkedIn profile appeared stellar but when I discovered the social side of this candidate and his activities—which turned out to be, shall we say, very nefarious things on Facebook and Instagram—it was clear he would not do well in this position.

Due to the ever-changing climate of online information management, effective personal brand management is more of a journey than a destination. So the next step is to create a proactive personal brand management strategy by following these steps:

First, make sure your **LinkedIn profile** is complete—and I mean REALLY COMPLETE! LinkedIn is now your résumé online and, unlike a paper résumé, you are NOT LIMITED by the amount of good content you can include in your profile. This includes testimonials, accomplishments, connections, videos, pictures, etc.

Second, make sure your **digital footprint** for your name search is filled with useful and positive information about you. Your digital footprint is the page-one Google results of searches for you by name. For example, my footprint can be found by typing "Dustin Ruge" in Google. If you have a more common name, you might need to include your geo and/or other descriptions to help narrow it down in the search for you. These first-page results will commonly include up to 15 different sources of information about you, including websites, pictures, videos, etc., so make sure you proactively monitor it to help ensure it is professional and will help you move forward in your career. In short, if you don't take control of your digital footprint, others will do it for you—and more often than not the results can be detrimental to you.

Third, if you have **negative information about you online,** find ways to push it off of the first page of Google. It may be possible to expunge negative information, but don't count on it—especially if it's coming from a news website that doesn't care about your opinion of their journalistic rights. The best thing you can do is create positive news from higher-authority websites and properties with the goal of pushing down and drowning out anything bad in the process. If the sites containing negative information allow you to respond to them, as many websites and review sites allow for today, make sure to provide your side of the story in a very professional way that will not sound spiteful but rather shows your professional side and ability to take the high road on such matters.

Finally, **monitor your results and be proactive.** The best way to monitor your branding results is to track them over time and trend the results. One of the first resources you should use to help you is Google Alerts, which can be accessed at Google.com/alerts. Google Alerts is free and allows you to create an alert for any brand name (including yours) so you can receive regular updates from Google any time your brand names are mentioned on the Internet, including blogs, media, video, books, etc. You can also set the frequency with which you receive these alerts. The default I always recommend to start with is weekly.

# CHAPTER 18

# RAISE MILLIONAIRE CHILDREN

• • •

*"Compound interest is the eighth wonder of the world.*
*He who understands it, earns it . . . he who doesn't . . . pays it."*
*— Albert Einstein*

I met Steven a few years back in his plush office in Beverly Hills, California. I knew when I walked into his office that this sales meeting was going to be different—and it was. His office was lined with oak paneling, thousands of books, and a desk normally seen in high-end furniture stores. As pretentious as his surroundings may have first appeared, Steven was anything but.

Our sales meeting lasted more than two hours, but I could tell that the time spent with him was worth it. Steven was in the later stages of his career as an attorney and businessman and had real estate holdings in the area rumored to be in excess of hundreds of millions of dollars. Despite his wealth, he still maintained a high-profile legal practice when most people would have decided that a comfortable retirement was a more appealing option. But not Steven.

At the conclusion of our sales meeting, I inquired about Steven's business acumen and, more specifically, his real estate holdings in the greater Los Angeles area.

"Steven, I've heard some of your peers speaking very fondly about your business savvy and, more specifically, how you got into real estate," I said. "I would love to hear your story if you're willing to share it with me."

"Dustin," replied Steven as he slowly sat back in his seat with a smile, "do you want to know how to get rich in America?"

"Of course," I replied as I leaned forward so as to not miss a sound of what could be coming my way.

"Good, because it's really pretty simple," said Steven. "You see, when I graduated law school, all my friends rewarded themselves by going out and buying new cars. I took that same money and bought my first corner property up in Woodland Hills instead. Over the years I continued to invest in more and more real estate instead of spending it on foolish things I didn't need to become wealthy."

"That's it?" I responded with a rather inquisitive look on my face, still waiting for the magical pearl of wisdom to come my way.

"No," said Steven with a smile. "The second part is to live long enough to have all those investments make you wealthy in the end like I have."

When Warren Buffett is asked what the single most important factor contributing to his success is his answer is always the same: "Compounding interest." Compounding interest is simply the ongoing interest earned on interest over time, which continues to multiply at higher levels the longer you reinvest (or hold) it. Buffett's own stock, Berkshire Hathaway, personifies this principle since it has reinvested all earnings and therefore has not paid dividends to its shareholders since Buffett took charge.

In many respects, both Steven and Warren have the same investment philosophy of buying, holding, reinvesting, and reaping the long-term rewards that made them both very wealthy. They both started adhering to this strategy early on in life and they both stayed disciplined to this strategy through both good times and bad. Most people paid little attention to the financial strategies of people like Steven and Warren until well into the later half of their lives. In fact, recent studies have shown that fully **80 percent of self-made millionaires became wealthy after the age of 50.**[1] It was not that they discovered how to save after the age of 50 but rather that was when compounding interest really started to pay off for them . . . because they lived long enough to see the fruits of their labor.

Unfortunately, people like Steven and Warren are rare in today's society, which increasingly promotes immediate gratification and rewards while shackling our younger generation with heavier loads of debt that rob them of their ability to grow wealth. But you have the chance to change that course for your own children starting today! Here are some ways to get started.

## HOW TO SAVE

Saving money early and habitually in life are fundamental traits shared by many self-made millionaires. Most self-made millionaires I know have a simple rule when it comes to savings: **15–20 percent of every dollar earned** is immediately placed into savings and/or investments and is not spent. The difference between deciding on fifteen or twenty percent is determined by how quickly you want to become a millionaire—the more you save early on, the faster the results.

For those who lack the discipline to *consistently* save by following this formula, you can always instruct your payroll company and/or bank to fund a specific bank/savings/investment account dedicated for this purpose. The sooner you and your children follow this process, the easier and more habitual it will become for both of you. And don't expect your children to instinctively do this on their own. Financial illiteracy runs rampant for most children well into their twenties, so this is your chance to be the great parent you always wanted to be!

## WHY WE SAVE

Here is an old riddle: If I offered you $3 million today or a penny each day that continued to double over thirty days, which one would you take? If you chose the penny option you would end up with $5 million in thirty days, or $2 million more than the instant gratification option of taking the money now. So which option would most people instinctively choose? This requires not only a bit of mathematical knowledge but also the ability to not suffer from two-dimensional thinking.

There is nothing initially "fun" about foregoing the instant gratification and rewards of spending unless you and, more important, your children know what saving will mean for your futures. Value in sales always comes down to the question of "compared to what?" and your job is to now sell the value of saving over spending to your children. Most comparisons of value are made against money, and as adults who have held jobs and earned money, you know what the true value of each dollar you own is worth to you. Your children likely don't yet have the same frame of reference.

So a good place to start is to lead by example. As previously discussed in this book, **children learn most by mirroring the habits of their parents—both good and bad.** According to studies, 75 percent of self-made millionaires indicated that they learned good success habits from their parents.[2] So the next time you start throwing money around like a drunken sailor in front of your children, don't be surprised when your children end up doing the same thing. You need to set a good "financial" example for your children to mirror and follow.

Once you clean up your own financial act around your kids, you next need to help educate them on the true value of money. This starts by teaching them the cost of earning money as opposed to simply giving it to them. There is an old proverb that if you give someone a fish today, you will have to give them another fish tomorrow. However, if you teach someone to fish, they can feed themselves forever. This proverb not only teaches the power of self-reliance, but it also gives context to a value exchange of work for rewards.

Some of the most successful people I know started out doing some of the least glamorous work in their foundational years. I will never forget one of my first "official" jobs working as a busboy at a local restaurant that was owned by a friend's father. Once I was able to see the real value of a dollar earned after doing "real" work and then paying Uncle Sam, my view of money was never the same again.

After my own experiences growing up, I developed a whole new outlook on money and savings and, more important, what saving can really earn you in life. If I were to sum it all up into one word, it would be **"freedom."**

**By saving at an early age, I earned:**

- The ability to decide where and who I wanted to work for in the future.

- Where I wanted to live and travel to in the future.

- What I wanted to become when I grew up.

- When I would quit my job and then move to be with my future wife when I wanted to. She thought I was crazy at the time for doing that.

- The ability to get the education I wanted.

- The ability to live the lifestyle I wanted to live.

- The ability to become an author and a public speaker.

- And much more . . .

So here's your chance to see just how good of a salesperson you are by asking these same questions of your children so you can help them understand the true value of money and what saving really earns them in their life ahead. To me, it has made all of the difference in the world and I know it will mean the same thing to your children as well.

## THE BURDEN OF PERSONAL DEBT

About a decade ago I went through a very painful divorce. Having two young children going through this process with me was something I wouldn't wish on anybody, including my worst enemies. But as I restarted my dating life, I began to see something I'd never quite experienced before. I began to meet people who had $50,000, $100,000, and even $150,000 in student loan debt—to pay for their undergraduate education!

As of the writing of this book, there are around 44 million Americans carrying a combined $1.3 billion of student loan debt. The average class of 2016 graduate now carries around $37,000 in student loan debt—which is more than many will earn their first year after graduation alone.[3]

The student loan business has grown dramatically since 1978 and along with it so have college tuition fees. Studies have shown that had these expansions and the subsequent tuition increases that followed the explosion in student loans not taken place, the cost of college would be half of what it is today.[4] Of course, a great deal of this debt was encouraged by our federal government, which is now $19 trillion in debt itself. The moral of this story is don't let your children mirror the behaviors of government . . . on many fronts, but especially when it comes to finances.

There is nothing more damaging to the future success, freedom, and happiness of your children than starting them out in their post-education years heavily in debt. **Economic mobility is a cornerstone of any free market economy and the more debt your children carry like a ball and chain tied to their leg, the more limited their mobility can become.** Andrew Jackson said it best: "When you get in debt you become a slave." Or to summarize Einstein's quote at the beginning of this chapter, you are either earning compounding interest or you are paying it. And the longer you are paying it by being in debt to others, the harder it will become to build wealth in your life and enjoy all the things it can earn you in the process.

To help avoid this debt trap, it's a good idea to consider all options to help your children avoid student debt. These can include setting up tax-free college savings accounts, working part-time while going to college, attending a community college for the first few years of their undergraduate work, looking for eligible scholarships/grants, taking advantage of employer tuition reimbursement programs, and much more.

## LEARN HOW TO CONTROL YOUR OWN VALUE

Your children will likely start their first working experiences by working for others—often for the least amount of money per hour they can legally be paid. If you want your children to learn and appreciate what they want in life, they need to start by learning what they don't want first. Remember: Working is like any decision and will always come down to the question "Compared to what?" You want that comparison to be stark, memorable, and foundational.

One of the earlier hourly jobs of my youth was working on a grounds crew at a very large sports and entertainment complex in Omaha, Nebraska, called AKSARBEN (that's Nebraska spelled backward . . . Catchy, isn't it?). Anyway, my first day on the job I was handed a Weed-wacker, a can of gas, and a jug of water, and dropped off for the rest of the day in a desolate field full of knee-high grass and weeds. I was being paid minimum wage by the hour to cut weeds and grass that day for eight hours straight. When the day was done, my shins were all cut up, I could barely move my arms, and I could hardly hear a thing as a result of that engine screaming near to my head all day.

The grounds manager who hired me later told me this was his way of determining if a new hire was tough enough to work there since most who weren't would simply quit after that first day in the fields. I came back to work the next day, and based on the initial expressions of the other workers—including the manager—when I walked back in, that was a rare sight to see.

Mowing hundreds of acres of lawn that summer provided me with a lot of time to think. But two things became crystal clear to me. First, I sure as hell didn't want to do this for the rest of my life, and second, I was no longer comfortable with other people putting a price on my time and work. I needed to find ways to create a higher value output for my time, otherwise I would always be paid nothing more than any other commodity. To do this, I needed to start mastering new skills.

As a child, the majority of your youth is dedicated to learning and experiencing new things. Most children are not yet aware of their "purpose in life" at this early age but they can begin to work on the other foundations of success, such as hard work, dedication, and mastering a skill.

The human brain is wired to learn and master certain activities through practice, repetition, constant refinement, and improvement.

The more hard work that is consistently dedicated to each of these areas surrounding a specific activity, the more valuable you can become to yourself and others. Now, most children are not going to have the time to dedicate 10,000 hours to master a skill as discussed in previous chapters, but there are ways they can start to master other activities with less time, thereby improving their position and earning more both now and in the future. And one of the best places to start is in sales.

One of the greatest aspects of sales is the ability it provides you to get paid for your performance and not just for your time. Once your children grasp this concept, you will help free them from this trap at an early age and will have taught them one of the most important foundational lessons in their work life ahead. They will be in good company as well, joining the likes of Warren Buffett, Mark Cuban, David Ogilvy, Mary Kay Ash, Dale Carnegie, Larry Ellison, and Reed Hastings, who all made the same choice at an early age to start in sales. Who knows; maybe your children will follow Buffett's lead and even claim their bicycles as a deduction on their tax returns . . . at age 13.[5]

# CHAPTER 19

# 14 STEPS TO TAKE ACTION NOW!

• • •

*"A goal without accountability is nothing more than a dream."*

Congratulations! You have (hopefully) made it through the entire book and are ready to start changing your life forever. If this describes you, then it's now time to take what you have learned and apply it to your success moving forward.

The following are 14 simple steps you can now take to get yourself on the road to becoming a millionaire salesperson.

## 1) DISCOVER YOUR PRIMARY PURPOSE

As discussed in chapter 2, the greatest power and results you can produce in your work come from your own passions—the more passion you have for what you do, the better your potential results in your career and in your life. In order to discover your passion, you need to start with awareness to determine what truly motivates you and makes you passionate and what does not.

To help discover your passions, think about the things that really "drive" and "self-motivate" you in life, such as hobbies; certain types of work; what you like to read, write about, or watch the most; people; family time; travel; etc. Ultimately these should be things that you love, that make you happy, and that you like spending your time doing. Put another way, **have you ever worked on something that you seem to**

**"lose track of time" or "run out of time" when doing it?** That could be one of your true passions.

On a final note, depending on your age and experiences, you may be at a point in your life where you have not yet experienced enough of the world to truly know what your passions are. If that describes you now, be patient and repeat this process again in the years that follow to see how your purpose may evolve as you live and learn.

On the lines below, write down your top five passions in life, with your greatest passions listed first:

1. Passion: _____

2. Passion: _____

3. Passion: _____

4. Passion: _____

5. Passion: _____

Now under each passion listed, write exactly what is needed (Dependencies) to fully achieve each passion in your life. Dependencies can commonly include things like specific levels of income and/or wealth, time, freedom, education, etc.

1. **Passion:** _____

    a. Dependency: _____

    b. Dependency: _____

    c. Dependency: _____

2. **Passion:** _____

    a. Dependency: _____

    b. Dependency: _____

    c. Dependency: _____

3. **Passion:** _____

    a. Dependency: _____

    b. Dependency: _____

c. Dependency: _____

4. **Passion:** _____

    a. Dependency: _____

    b. Dependency: _____

    c. Dependency: _____

5. **Passion:** _____

    a. Dependency: _____

    b. Dependency: _____

    c. Dependency: _____

## 2) SETTING YOUR SUCCESSFUL GOALS

As we discussed in chapter 5, goal setting allows you to define success and then discover how to laser-focus on achieving it. The best goals are written goals that you hold yourself accountable for through the use of regular reflection. In many respects, your goals may simply be the definition of your Dependencies and/or a time frame in which they are achieved. For example, your Dependency may be to become a millionaire while your goal may be to earn at least $5 million by the age of 50.

Now, under each Dependency you created under each Passion, write exactly what goals are needed to fully achieve each Dependency.

1. **Passion:** _____

    a. Dependency: _____

        i. Goal: _____

        ii. Goal: _____

        iii. Goal: _____

    b. Dependency: _____

        i. Goal: _____

        ii. Goal: _____

        iii. Goal: _____

c. Dependency: _____
    i. Goal: _____
    ii. Goal: _____
    iii. Goal: _____

Now repeat this process for each Passion and its relative Dependencies you want to potentially consider and pursue.

## 3) DEFINE YOUR NUMBERS

As discussed in chapter 4, all success has a number, and those numbers should be broken down into daily (keystone) activities. Once you have written down your Passions, Dependencies, and Goals, it is time to define those Goals by breaking them down into daily (keystone) activities.

1. **Passion:** _____

    a. Dependency: _____

        i. Goal: _____

            1. Daily Activity:_____
            2. Daily Activity:_____
            3. Daily Activity:_____

        ii. Goal: _____

            1. Daily Activity:_____
            2. Daily Activity:_____
            3. Daily Activity:_____

        iii. Goal: _____

            1. Daily Activity:_____
            2. Daily Activity:_____
            3. Daily Activity:_____

Now repeat this process for each Goal under each relative Dependency and Passion you want to potentially consider and pursue.

# 4) START BUILDING SUCCESSFUL SALES HABITS

As we discussed in chapter 3, great growth businesses are built on great systems, and great salespeople are no different. In order to be successful and increase your own success, you have to create your own internal success systems in the form of habits. Once these good habits are created and bad habits removed, your ability, effectiveness, and results will improve with it.

The first step in the process is to identify both the good and bad habits you will need to help support and promote your Daily Activities you previously defined above. Please refer to chapter 3 for a list of the most common good and bad habits.

1. Goal: _____

    a. Daily Activity: _____

        i. Habit: _____

        ii. Habit: _____

        iii. Habit: _____

Next, you will need to define the keystone activities that are needed to help support good habits and/or break your bad habits. As discussed in chapter 3, keystone habits such as exercise, sleep, diet, saving money, etc., can impact multiple habits at the same time like a domino effect.

1. Goal: _____

    a. Daily Activity: _____

        i. Habit: _____

            1. Keystone Habit:_____

        ii. Habit: _____

            1. Keystone Habit:_____

        iii. Habit: _____

            1. Keystone Habit:_____

Now that you have identified your habits and keystone habits needed to produce all of the results leading to your Passions, you can put a 60–90 day habit-forming process in place like we discussed in chapter 3, and check your results.

Here is an example of how a completed list may look based on somebody else's Passions:

**1. Passion:** (Collect Antique Cars)

    **a. Dependencies:** (High levels of disposable income)

        **i. Goal:** (Earn at least $150K/year after taxes and living expenses)

            **1. Daily Activity:** (Close an average of $3,300 in sales per day)

                **i. Habit:** (Conduct at least 3 sales meetings per day)

                    **a. Keystone Habit:** (Wake up at 5 a.m. each morning and rigidly follow a daily schedule)

                    **b. Keystone Habit:** (30 minutes of exercise each morning)

                    **c. Keystone Habit:** (Completing a daily sales activity checklist each day)

                **ii. Habit:** (Make at least 120 sales prospecting phone calls per day)

                    **a. Keystone Habit:** (Complete a daily sales activity checklist each day)

                    **b. Keystone Habit:** (Say "NO" to any activity/distraction that is not pre-scheduled for my day ahead)

                    **c. Etc...**

## 5) MAXIMIZE YOUR LIMITED TIME

As discussed in chapter 6, time management and knowing what your time is worth is critical to your sales growth and success in business. Only when you know the value of your own time and the fact that it is always limited can you truly maximize and create more of it by buying other people's time to add to it.

To do this, **you first need to calculate what each hour of your work time is worth based on your income goal for the year** (see chart in chapter 6 for reference). This is calculated by dividing your annual income goal ($_____) by your total hours worked (2,350), giving you your cost per hour ($_____). Now you know what the cost for your time on an hourly basis should be. For example, in chapter 6, Linda calculated her cost per hour ($85) by dividing her annual income target ($200,000) by the total average hours worked per year (2,350).

Next you need to identify and help remove all of the ways you are less productive in your current work by writing them down and then taking steps to eliminate them from your limited working hours. These can commonly include time wasted on distractions, commuting, poor organizational skills, sales support activities, when you start your work day, not following a daily schedule and plan, etc.

List below the top five ways you are currently less productive today (see chapter 6 for examples):

1. _____

2. _____

3. _____

4. _____

5. _____

Now that you have taken steps to help identify and improve your productivity, it's time to add more time and productivity to your work by buying more time from other people. In order to do this, you need to list all of your daily activities in your work, their time requirements, who else could do them other than you, what they cost, and then calculate the impacts on you and your business (see chapter 6 for examples and calculations).

| DAILY TASK REASSIGNMENT LIST (EXAMPLE) | | | | | |
|---|---|---|---|---|---|
| Activity | Time (in-Hours) | Can be Completed by Support (Yes/No)? | Support Needed (By Name/Title) | Support Cost (per Hour Worked) | Support Cost per Day |
| | | | | $ | $ |
| | | | | $ | $ |
| | | | | $ | $ |
| | | | | $ | $ |
| | | | | $ | $ |
| | | | | $ | $ |
| | | | | $ | $ |
| | | | | $ | $ |
| | | | | $ | $ |
| | | | | $ | $ |
| Totals: | | | | | $ |

## 6) EXERCISE YOUR BODY AND YOUR MIND

As discussed in chapters 7 and 8, your body and your mind are the engines of your own success and you need to regularly exercise and feed both if you are going to succeed in both sales and your career ahead. Here are the most common ways to do this now:

☑ Educationally read no less than 30 minutes each day. Find and schedule time to read without distractions.

☑ Leverage your customers, networks, and mentors to constantly learn more from them. Ask a lot of questions and seek out advice. There is no need to reinvent the wheel when you can learn from those who already have at their own time and expense.

☑Exercise at least 30 minutes each day—typically at the beginning of your day if possible as it will help improve your attitude and performance throughout the day.

☑Develop good sleep habits and schedule your sleep time for no less than 7 to 8 hours per night. Remember: How well you sleep has a direct impact on how you learn and your productivity when you are awake—one feeds the other.

☑Love what you sell and don't settle—the more you believe in what you are selling and why you are selling it, the better salesperson you can become.

☑Always strive to work with a positive attitude. Remember, selling is all about the attitude of the seller, not the buyer. Attitude (both positive and negative) is also contagious, so your sales will typically be at their best when your attitude is at its best.

## 7) LEARN TO CLOSE EVERY DEAL

If you are in sales, don't confuse selling for closing. Since most salespeople still hesitate and fail to ask for a close, you are already ahead of the game once you realize that your ultimate job is to close—period!

Here are some steps/tips you can take to help you close more business in your sales ahead:

☑Always remember that 70 percent of people buy out of fear while only 30 percent buy to gain something. Unless you are addressing the fears of not buying your product or service, you are not selling to why the majority of people end up making (or not making) buying decisions.

☑The final decision to buy is an emotional, not a rational, decision, so when they are ready to decide, stop selling rationally to your buyers and appeal to their emotions instead.

☑Remember that most people buy want they want—not what they need. Your job is not to uncover and sell to their needs but rather to get them to want what you are trying to sell.

☑Always remember the Five Whys of Closing that every buyer will ask themselves (consciously or not) and why it is important to follow the sequence of these questions in your sales process as well. These include: **WHY YOU? WHY YOUR COMPANY? WHY CHANGE? WHY YOUR PRODUCT/SERVICE?** And **WHY NOW?** See chapter 9 for more details about the Five Whys of Closing and what you need to know and do during each phase of this process to close more sales.

☑ Always help proactively answer the "Compared to what?" question for each of your sales prospects. Once you can provide your buyers with a basis of superior comparative value, define their options in advance, reframe your value, and make your products and services easier to buy and sell you will be able to close more business and move the majority of your buyers past the easiest decision they can make—which is to do nothing!

## 8) BECOME A MASTER STORYTELLER

As we discussed in chapter 11, people cannot learn anything without applying meaning to it, and the most effective way to grab your buyer's attention, have them remember and understand what you said, and compel them to buy is through effective storytelling.

Here are some steps/tips you can use to help you create and utilize storytelling in your sales ahead:

☑ Create stories that will help support the most critical phases of your sales process. These include:

> • Customer introduction stories: These stories help you get past the "why you" and "why your company" concerns that are initially on the minds of your customers.
> • In-common customer success stories: These stories help you get past the "why change" and "why your product/service" questions that are in the minds of your customers.
> • Common customer objection stories: These stories help you overcome sales objections and will also help you get past the "why now" questions that are in the minds of your customers.

☑ Always try to structure your stories based on "the hero's journey" with the key sequential elements being:

- The setup/setting
- The confrontation/conflict
- The mentor (YOU!)
- The resolution/transformation

☑Use simple but powerful visuals to help support your stories. Remember, people think in images, not words, because visuals help create structure and meaning to words.

☑Regularly document and update your customer success stories for easy recall, access, sharing, and use. Ideally you should have three stories created for each category (nine total).

## 9) START BUILDING YOUR SUCCESS NETWORK TODAY

As discussed in chapter 12, millionaires look for and build networks while everybody else looks for work. As our society continues to grow in size and complexity, you need to constantly build up these zones of trust and influence to help you sell and advance your career. Here are a few of the ways you can help accomplish this:

☑Create leverage by identifying and accessing key herd leaders who can help you more rapidly gain access and sway over strategic networks and groups that can help you.

☑Utilize the power of reciprocity to more quickly gain access and trust with key people and sales prospects. To maximize your results, make sure that your reciprocity is **Unexpected, Unique,** and **Personalized.**

☑Identify and learn from career mentors. Why make the same mistakes others have made before you and learned from already when you can learn them in advance from your mentors? Mentors can help you overcome these hurdles, provide access to key people, and help you get ahead faster in your career.

☑Leverage your network for referrals. A strong referral can lead to many things, including warmer leads, higher close rates, and more sales. Great salespeople know how to turn their networks into powerful sales conversion engines.

## 10) BUILD A WINNING PERSONAL BRAND

As discuss in chapter 13, the first and arguably the most important brand you first have to sell in any sales situation is yourself. Great salespeople are great for a reason and will find ways to become successful in nearly every place they work. That is why they are so highly sought after by employers. So here are some of the key ways you can help build up your own personal brand:

☑Dedicate yourself to becoming an expert at what you do by creating a five-year expert sales plan. People are not born into greatness—most people have to work hard to ultimately achieve it in life. Ten thousand hours seems to be the magic number, and since most people only work 2,350 hours a year, start planning on 4–5 years before you can reach a point of greatness in your work.

☑Help others properly introduce you. Once you create a strong brand, make sure people know exactly how to present you to others—the stronger the introduction, the greater the potential level of immediate credibility and trust you will receive—leading to higher sales!

☑Find ways to more quickly build levels of trust and respect with others. Most people today will formulate their first impressions about you in less than three seconds, so train yourself to always smile at people when you first meet them and avoid selling to others when you are in a bad mood.

☑Project success for others to see and help judge you by. Remember that people are not going to give you their money if you don't look like you know what to do with it. A good part of what people decide if they want to buy from you or not comes from how you dress, your manners and appearance, your posture and confidence, and how you communicate with others.

## 11) BUILD AND FOLLOW YOUR SALES SYSTEM

As discussed in chapter 15, the majority of businesses today still do not have a defined sales process, and even if they do, it may not always be as successful as the one you can create for yourself. Great salespeople will create a sales processes for themselves that is standardized, repeatable, and scalable—the better and more refined the system is, the better the potential results.

Each business and sales situation can be unique, so it is important to start with the basics, document your system, and refine as you go. If you need to create a sales system for yourself and/or your business, please read chapter 15 for more details.

## 12) KNOW YOUR CUSTOMERS

As discussed in chapter 16, not every customer is the right customer for you and your business. The sooner you grasp this concept and create a system to better manage it, the more successful you will be in sales. Here are a few key steps you can take in this process:

☑Create a Target Client Profile (or avatar) for you and your company to sell and market to. Once you have created your customer avatar, make sure to publish it for all in your business to see, and refer to it often (see example in chapter 16).

☑Focus your time and interests on customers who will help you sell while avoiding those who won't. As discussed in chapter 16, there are only three types of clients you will ever sell to: Promoters, Buyers, and Demoters. In order to maximize your results, you need to be able to classify each sales prospect and customer based on these three types and then strategically manage your time around them.

☑Learn how to say "NO" to bad customers. The easiest way to be able to do this is to first develop a system that produces more potential Promoter and Buyer customers than you can handle, then classify and quickly qualify these sales leads, and most important, know who to say "no" to during the sales process.

## 13) PLAN FOR JOB CHANGES NOW

As discussed in chapter 17, the only constant in today's business world is change and you should never confuse your job with your career. If your career is in sales, it is very likely you will work in multiple jobs throughout your career, so it is important that you start preparing for these changes now so your career is always moving in the right direction despite any bad jobs you may have along the way. Here are a few key ways to help make this happen:

- ☑ Start personally saving your money with the goal of having at least 6–12 months of your regular income saved for career mobility as soon as possible. Nothing will set your career back more than being stuck in a dead-end job because you didn't have the financial resources and mobility ready to help support a necessary job change.
- ☑ Create multiple streams of income with the eventual goal of having up to three different income sources to help support you and your family throughout your career. See chapter 17 for more details and suggestions.
- ☑ Make sure to take control of and constantly improve your own digital footprint online for others to see. If you are a successful salesperson, most companies and recruiters will be actively looking for people like you online, and the stronger and more visible your brand is, the more career opportunities will come your way. See chapter 17 for more details and suggestions.

## 14) PLAN AND INVEST FOR THE FUTURE

As discussed in chapter 18, there are many ways to become a millionaire but one of the most effective ways to accomplish this is through the use of compounding interest. Far too many children today grow up financially illiterate only to learn later in life that compounding interest can pay the highest returns the earlier in life that you start using it.

There are a number of ways you and members of your family can learn and adopt these concepts in your own lives. Here are a few key areas to start:

- ☑ Create a habit and system of saving and investing 15–20 percent of each dollar you ever earn. Apply this same principle to your children as well so they can start learning how to save and live within their means at an early age.

☑Set a proper financial example for your children to follow. Most children grow up heavily influenced by the actions and habits of their parents. So don't expect your children to simply "learn from your financial mistakes" when most will likely be doomed to repeat them if you don't set the right examples for them to follow starting now.

☑Find ways to avoid saddling you and your children with the burden of financial debt. Teach your children to earn before they spend and how to make wise decisions that won't prevent them from having maximum career mobility after their formal education is completed.

☑Teach your children how to earn money so they will understand at an early age the value and true cost of acquiring money and the best ways to earn more of it throughout their lives. Like most people, your children will initially need to start out by being paid an hourly wage and working one or more undesirable jobs. This will help them truly know what they don't want to do and will help them answer through experience the question "Compared to what?" in their own minds.

☑Teach your children how to build up their own unique personal value and how to use critical thinking when making work and career decisions. This will help free them from the hourly-wage trap and help them to earn more based on their performance instead of their time. One of the easiest ways to accomplish this is through sales— starting at an early age!

# EPILOGUE

● ● ●

*"Everyone thinks of changing the world,*
*but no one thinks of changing himself."*
— Leo Tolstoy

A number of years have passed since I first met Linda. Since our time working together, she has found purpose, focus, and success in her life and her career. As a result, Linda quickly transitioned from a person of envy and anguish to consistently being one of the top performers in her career. But Linda was not alone in this accomplishment; I have witnessed the same type of transformation countless times during the decades of my work with sales professionals.

One of the most rewarding aspects of sales is the ability to work with and help dramatically improve the lives of others. My own rewards and motivations over the years have evolved from the customer to include sales professionals like Linda, putting me in a position where I can move beyond a sales transaction and make an even greater impact in the lives of others. This has also allowed me to forge lifelong relationships that continue to enrich my life greatly and help serve my own purpose.

But just as Linda and others have found great success in sales, I have also learned that not everybody is cut out to be a great salesperson. To help illustrate this point, I frequently remind others that you cannot teach a mule to win the Kentucky Derby. No matter how much you teach them, no matter how much they know, they will never become a thoroughbred.

As a sales manager and coach, my role in helping people like Linda to improve their sales performance can also carry equal weight in my determination of whether or not they have the foundational character needed to succeed in sales to begin with. So how can you help identify these characteristics for yourself? That is why I wrote my first book, *The Successful Sales Manager: A Sales Manager's Handbook for Building Great Sales Performance*—to help others answer this question for themselves.

I truly believe God has provided each and every one of us with unique gifts and qualities—some of which are well suited for a successful career in sales while many are not. Often the ability to make this determination alone can be the difference between a great salesperson and a great sales manager.

I recently visited with another sales protégé like Linda more than a decade after we first started working together. Much like Linda, Steve was also struggling until he too decided to look within and change himself for the better. Not only did Steve become a highly successful salesperson, but his newly found career mobility led him on a career path that vastly improved his compensation and fortunes as well. And his success has not gone unnoticed.

Steve now likes to tell me that not only will he outearn the highest paid executives at his company each year but that his ability to now project his success for others to easily find and see has made him a target for high-end sales recruiters who approach him frequently with job offers that most other salespeople would only dream of. Clearly Steve's success now transcends his current job and has developed into a highly successful career full of seemingly endless future opportunities. All of this has helped change everything about Steve's life and, just as important, the future of Steve's family and those who depend on him as well.

On a final note, everybody at one time in their life dreams of "changing the world" and imagines what life could be like for themselves and others as a result. We live in a society where we marvel at the accomplishments of others who in many ways did change the world as we know it today, but we forget that those changes all started somewhere much smaller and internally before they ended up impacting the world around us.

You and everyone around you has the ability to help change the world for the better, and for many, a successful career in sales can become the keystone event in your life that can help make this all happen for you—just as it has for Linda and many other people like her. But in order to change the world, you will need to start from within and change yourself first. That is why I wrote this book—and if you and others like you can continue to improve your lives as a result, then let's start changing the world together!

# NOTES AND REFERENCES

• • •

## Introduction

1. "The Difference Between Good and Great." *People V. The State of Illusion Blog,* October 21, 2012. http://thestateofillusion.com/2012/10/the-difference-between-good-and-great/ (accessed October 16, 2016).

2. "PGA Tour Money Leaders 2015." ESPN PGA Golf, http://www.espn.com/golf/moneylist/_/page/1/year/2015 (accessed October 16, 2016).

3. Michael Bosworth, 2012. *What Great Salespeople Do: The Science of Selling Through Emotional Connection and the Power of Story,* (New York: McGraw-Hill Companies), 7.

## Chapter 1: Understanding the Sales Paradox

1. Eric Savitz, 2011. "The Path to Becoming a Fortune 500 CEO." *Forbes.* https://www.forbes.com/sites/ciocentral/2011/12/05/the-path-to-becoming-a-fortune-500-ceo/ (accessed September 12, 2016).

2. Alison Doyle, 2016. "Top 15 Kids' Dream Jobs." The Balance. https://www.thebalance.com/top-kids-dream-jobs-2062280 (accessed September 18, 2016).

3. Vickie Elmer, 2012. "30% of People End Up Working in the Careers They Dreamed of as Kids." *Quartz Media.* https://qz.com/29058/workers-outside-the-us-are-more-likely-to-pursue-their-dream-jobs/ (accessed September 20, 2016).

## Chapter 2: What Is Your Primary Purpose?

1. Bronnie Ware, 2015. "Regrets of the Dying." http://www.bronnieware.com/blog/regrets-of-the-dying (accessed September 14, 2016).

2. Howard Farran, 2015. *Uncomplicate Business: All It Takes Is People, Time, and Money,* (Austin: Greenleaf Group Press), 33.

3. Douglas Belkin, 2017. "Exclusive Test Data: Many Colleges Fail To Improve Critical-Thinking Skills." *The Wall Street Journal.* https://www.wsj.com/articles/exclusive-test-data-many-colleges-fail-to-improve-critical-thinking-skills-1496686662 (accessed June 6, 2017).

## Chapter 3: Building "Personal" Sales Systems Through Habits

1. Ray Kroc, 1977. *Grinding It Out: The Making of McDonalds.* (New York: St. Martin's Press).

2. Tom Corley, 2016. *Change Your Habits, Change Your Life: Strategies That Transformed 177 Average People into Self-Made Millionaires* (Minneapolis: North Loop Books), 4.

3. Dr. Michel Royon, 2016. "The Human Brain Is Loaded Daily With 34 GB of Information." Tech 21 Century. https://www.tech21century.com/the-human-brain-is-loaded-daily-with-34-gb-of-information/ (accessed December 29, 2016).

4. Tom Corley, 2016. *Change Your Habits, Change Your Life: Strategies That Transformed 177 Average People into Self-Made Millionaires* (Minneapolis: North Loop Books), 13.

5. Benjamin Franklin Quotes, 2016. BrainyQuote https://www.brainyquote.com/quotes/quotes/b/benjaminfr151624.html (accessed November 12, 2016).

6. CSO Insights, 2016. "2016 CSO Insight Sales Best Practices Study." https://www.csoinsights.com/wp-content/uploads/sites/5/2016/08/Sales-Best-Practice-Study.pdf (accessed June 2, 2017).

7. Tom Corley, 2016. *Change Your Habits, Change Your Life: Strategies That Transformed 177 Average People into Self-Made Millionaires* (Minneapolis: North Loop Books), 7.

## Chapter 4: Success Always Has a Number

1. Joe Girard with Stanley H. Brown, 2005. *How to Sell Anything to Anybody* (New York: FIRESIDE).

2. Ibid.

3. Ibid.

## Chapter 5: Personal Goals—Setting Your Path to Success

1. Tom Corley, 2016. *Change Your Habits, Change Your Life: Strategies That Transformed 177 Average People into Self-Made Millionaires* (Minneapolis: North Loop Books), 55.

2. Mark H. McCormack, 1984. *What They Don't Teach You at Harvard Business School* (New York: Bantam Books).

3. Greg McKeown, 2012. "The Disciplined Pursuit of Less." *Harvard Business Review: HBR Blog Network.* blogs.hbr.org/2012/08/the-disciplined-pursuit-of-less/ (accessed April 2, 2014).

## Chapter 6: Stop Wasting Your Time!

1. Gerhard Gschwandtner, 2011. "How Much Time Do Your Salespeople Spend Selling?" *Selling Power Blog.* http://blog.sellingpower.com/gg/2011/02/how-much-time-do-your-salespeople-spend-selling.html (accessed June 21, 2016).

2. Tom Corley, 2016. *Change Your Habits, Change Your Life: Strategies That Transformed 177 Average People into Self-Made Millionaires* (Minneapolis: North Loop Books), 91.

3. Best Jobs: Receptionist Salary, 2016. "How Much Do Receptionist Make?" *U.S. News & World Report Rankings.* https://money.usnews.com/careers/best-jobs/receptionist/salary (accessed June 13, 2017).

4. Tom Corley, 2016. *Change Your Habits, Change Your Life: Strategies That Transformed 177 Average People into Self-Made Millionaires* (Minneapolis: North Loop Books), 112.

5. Jennifer Ackerman, 2007. *Sex Sleep Eat Drink Dream: A Day In The Life Of Your Body* (New York: Houghton Mifflin Harcourt Publishing Company).

6. Tom Corley, 2016. *Change Your Habits, Change Your Life: Strategies That Transformed 177 Average People into Self-Made Millionaires* (Minneapolis: North Loop Books) 38–39.

7. Christopher Ingraham, 2016. "The Astonishing Human Potential Wasted on Commutes." *The Washington Post.* https://www.washingtonpost.com/news/wonk/wp/2016/02/25/how-much-of-your-life-youre-wasting-on-your-commute/ (accessed April 12, 2016).

8. "Warren Buffett Biography—Documentary." Posted by "I'm a millionaire." YouTube, 2012. https://www.youtube.com/watch?v=rLXtRjfVwcw (accessed July 22, 2016).

9. Chris Bailey, 2014. "Here's Why You Procrastinate, and 10 Tactics That Will Help You Stop." A Life of Productivity. http://alifeofproductivity.com/why-you-procrastinate-10-tactics-to-help-you-stop/ (accessed May 29, 2016).

10. Geoffrey James, 2015. "New Study: The Average Worker Now Spends 30 Hours a Week Checking Email." *Inc.* https://www.inc.com/geoffrey-james/new-study-the-average-worker-spends-30-hours-a-week-checking-email.html (accessed September 12, 2016).

11. Arielle Tambini, Nicolas Ketz, Lila Davachi, 2010. "Enhanced Brain Correlations During Rest Are Related to Memory for Recent Experiences." *Neuron.* http://www.cell.com/neuron/abstract/S0896-6273%2810%2900006-1 (accessed June 2, 2016).

## Chapter 7: Exercise the Mind

1. Gary Wu, 2014. "How Reading Impacted Warren Buffett, Marc Cuban, and Malcom X." http://www.garywu.net/influential-people-importance-reading/ (accessed July 14, 2016).

2. Michael Simmons, Ian Chew, Shizuka Ebata, 2016. "Bill Gates, Warren Buffett, and Oprah Winfrey All Use the 5-Hour Rule." *Inc.* https://www.inc.com/empact/bill-gates-warren-buffett-and-oprah-all-use-the-5-hour-rule.html (accessed September 17, 2016).

3. Tom Corley, 2016. *Change Your Habits, Change Your Life: Strategies That Transformed 177 Average People into Self-Made Millionaires* (Minneapolis: North Loop Books), 52, 92.

4. Claire Kolumban, 2016. "Seven Personality Traits of Top Salespeople." The Painless Business Stack. https://blog.gonimbly.com/seven-per-sonality-traits-of-top-salespeople-16c73845af73 (accessed July 17, 2016).

## Chapter 8: Build Energy, Attitude, and Passion

1. "Warren Buffett's Career Advice." *Fortune.* Posted by "CNN Money." YouTube, 2012. https://www.youtube.com/watch?v=8aNKhVPKHBc (accessed July 22, 2016).

2. Patrick Morris, 2014. "Warren Buffett Reveals the Simple Secret to His Success." The Motley Fool. https://www.fool.com/investing/general/2014/03/16/warren-buffett-reveals-the-simple-secrets-to-his-s.aspx (accessed July 24, 2016).

3. Emma Brudner, 2014. "The Majority of Salespeople Are Looking for a New Job." Hubspot. https://blog.hubspot.com/sales/salespeople-looking-for-new-job-infographic#sm.0001786vfdc7ydtaxjh2cy491orur (accessed July 24, 2016).

4. Carmine Gallo, 2013. "How Southwest and Virgin American Win by Putting People Before Profit." *Forbes.* https://www.forbes.com/sites/carminegallo/2013/09/10/how-southwest-and-virgin-america-win-by-putting-people-before-profit/ (accessed July 26, 2016).

5. "Coca-Cola: Happiness Starts With A Smile." 2015. https://www.youtube.com/watch?v=1veWbLpGa78&t=1s (accessed July 27, 2016).

6. Pamela Gerloff, 2011. "You're Not Laughing Enough, and That's No Joke." *Psychology Today.* https://www.psychologytoday.com/blog/the-possibility-paradigm/201106/youre-not-laughing-enough-and-thats-no-joke (accessed June 21, 2016).

7. Dr. Stanley Coren, 2009. "Smarter Than You Think: Renowned Canine Researcher Puts Dogs' Intelligence on Par with 2-Year-Old Human." American Psychological Association. http://www.apa.org/news/press/releases/2009/08/dogs-think.aspx (accessed June 12, 2016).

8. Michael Bosworth, 2012. *What Great Salespeople Do: The Science of Selling Through Emotional Connection and the Power of Story* (New York: McGraw-Hill Companies), 28.

9. Carmine Gallo, 2013. "How Southwest and Virgin American Win by Putting People Before Profit." *Forbes.* https://www.forbes.com/sites/carminegallo/2013/09/10/how-southwest-and-virgin-america-win-by-putting-people-before-profit/ (accessed July 26, 2016).

10. Tom Corley, 2016. *Change Your Habits, Change Your Life: Strategies That Transformed 177 Average People into Self-Made Millionaires* (Minneapolis: North Loop Books), 53.

11. Daniel H. Pink, 2012. *To Sell Is Human: The Surprising Truth About Moving Others* (New York: Riverhead Books), 16.

12. Ryan Fuller, 2015. "What Makes Great Salespeople." *Harvard Business Review.* https://hbr.org/2015/07/what-makes-great-sales-people (accessed June 12, 2016).

13. Tom Corley, 2016. *Change Your Habits, Change Your Life: Strategies That Transformed 177 Average People into Self-Made Millionaires* (Minneapolis: North Loop Books), 63.

14. Alice Schroeder, 2009. *The Snowball: Warren Buffett and The Business of Life* (New York: Bantam Books).

15. Tom Corley, 2016. *Change Your Habits, Change Your Life: Strategies That Transformed 177 Average People into Self-Made Millionaires* (Minneapolis: North Loop Books), 57.

16. Christine Hsu, 2012. "Nearly a Third of Americans Are Sleep Deprived." *Medical Daily.* http://www.medicaldaily.com/nearly-third-americans-are-sleep-deprived-240273 (accessed June 12, 2016).

17. John Medina, 2008. *Brain Rules: 12 Principles for Surviving and Thriving at Work, Home, and School* (Seattle: Pear Press).

18. Andrea Petersen, 2016. "The Unexpected Ways Sleep Deprivation Makes Life Tougher." *The Wall Street Journal.* https://www.wsj.com/articles/the-unexpected-ways-sleep-deprivation-makes-life-tougher-1473698556 (accessed July 7, 2016).

19. Judah Pollack & Olivia Fox Cabane, 2016. "Your Brain Has A 'Delete' Button—Here's How To Use It." *Fast Company.* https://www.fastcompany.com/3059634/your-brain-has-a-delete-button-heres-how-to-use-it (accessed July 8, 2016).

## Chapter 9: Coffee Is for Closers

1. BuzzBuilder Lead Generation Software, 2013. "20 Shocking Sales Stats That Will Change How You Sell." Slideshare. www.slideshare.net/JakeAtwood1/20-shocking-sales-stats (accessed March 8, 2014).

2. Ibid.

3. "Prospect Theory." *Wikipedia*. https://en.wikipedia.org/wiki/Prospect_theory (accessed June 6, 2016).

4. "The Golden Circle Clip." TED: Simon Sinek—"The Golden Circle" Clip. Posted by "Nelson Holmes." YouTube, 2012. www.youtube.com/watch?v=l5Tw0PGcyN0 (accessed June 28, 2016).

5. Michael Bosworth, 2012. *What Great Salespeople Do: The Science of Selling Through Emotional Connection and the Power of Story* (New York: McGraw-Hill Companies), 112.

### Chapter 10: Compared to What?

1. Sheena Iyengar, 2011. "How to Make Choosing Easier." TED Talks. https://www.ted.com/talks/sheena_iyengar_choosing_what_to_choose#t-913726 (accessed June 6, 2016).

2. Patrick Spenner & Karen Freeman, 2012. "To Keep Your Customers, Keep it Simple." *Harvard Business Review*. https://hbr.org/2012/05/to-keep-your-customers-keep-it-simple (accessed June 27, 2016).

3. Traffic Safety Facts, 2015. "Critical Reasons For Crashes Investigated in the National Motor Vehicle Crash Causation Survey." National Highway Traffic Safety Council. https://crashstats.nhtsa.dot.gov/Api/Public/ViewPublication/812115 (accessed June 28, 2016).

4. Patrick Spenner & Karen Freeman, 2012. "To Keep Your Customers, Keep it Simple." *Harvard Business Review*. https://hbr.org/2012/05/to-keep-your-customers-keep-it-simple (accessed June 27, 2016).

5. Geoffrey A. Fowler, 2017. "When 4.3 Stars Is Average: The Internet's Grade Inflation Problem." *The Wall Street Journal*. https://www.wsj.com/articles/when-4-3-stars-is-average-the-internets-grade-inflation-problem-1491414200 (accessed June 28, 2017).

6. Ibid.

7. Lindsay Konsko, 2014. "Credit Cards Make You Spend More: Studies." NerdWallet. https://www.nerdwallet.com/blog/credit-cards/credit-cards-make-you-spend-more/ (accessed June 8, 2016).

8. Gregory Ciotti, 2016. "10 Ways to Convert More Customers Using Psychology." Help Scout. https://www.helpscout.net/consumer-behavior/ (accessed June 12, 2016).

9. Joe Girard with Stanley H. Brown, 2005. *How to Sell Anything to Anybody* (New York: FIRESIDE).

## Chapter 11: People Who Tell Stories Rule the World

1. Scott Tousley, 2015. "107 Mind-Blowing Sales Statistics That Will Help You Sell Smarter." Hubspot. https://blog.hubspot.com/sales/sales-statistics (accessed July 17, 2016).

2. Joe Lynch, 2015. "3PL Sales: Hunting vs. Farming." The Logistics of Logistics. http://www.thelogisticsoflogistics.com/3pl_sales_hunting_vs_farming/ (accessed July 18, 2016).

3. Chadwick Martin Bailey, 2013. "25 Mind Blowing Email Marketing Stats." *Salesforce Blog.* https://www.salesforce.com/blog/2013/07/email-marketing-stats.html (accessed July 19, 2016).

4. "Show Trivia, #6." 2012. Magnum Mania. http://magnum-mania.com/Trivia/Trivia.html (accessed July 18, 2016).

5. Tim Riesterer, 2016. "Is the '57 Percent Stat' an Urban Legend?" Corporate Visions. https://corporatevisions.com/is-the-57-percent-stat-an-urban-legend/ (accessed December 28, 2016).

6. Ritu Pant, 2015. "Visual Marketing: A Picture's Worth 60,000 Words." Business 2 Community. http://www.business2community.com/digital-marketing/visual-marketing-pictures-worth-60000-words-01126256#PKVPUsESMhVa5wwP.97 (accessed July 18, 2016).

## Chapter 12: Build Success Networks

1. Anna Mar, 2013. "48 Selling Tips from the King of Advertising." *Simplicable.* http://business.simplicable.com/business/new/48-selling-tips-from-the-king-of-advertising (accessed March 13, 2016).

2. Tom Corley, 2016. *Change Your Habits, Change Your Life: Strategies That Transformed 177 Average People into Self-Made Millionaires* (Minneapolis: North Loop Books), 13.

3. Sheree Johnson, 2014. "New Research Sheds Light on Daily Ad Exposure." SJ Insights. https://sjinsights.net/2014/09/29/new-research-sheds-light-on-daily-ad-exposures/ (accessed March 17, 2016).

4. Scott Tousley, 2015. "107 Mind-Blowing Sales Statistics That Will Help You Sell Smarter." Hubspot. https://blog.hubspot.com/sales/sales-statistics (accessed July 17, 2016).

5. Tom Corley, 2016. *Change Your Habits, Change Your Life: Strategies That Transformed 177 Average People into Self-Made Millionaires* (Minneapolis: North Loop Books), 45.

**Chapter 13: Make Yourself Stand Out**

1. Tom Riley, 2008. "First Impression: When You Can't Compete on Price." *NAHAD News.* http://www.nahad.org/aws/nahad/asset_manager/get_file/36375 (accessed January 21, 2015).

2. "Outliers (book)." *Wikipedia.* https://en.wikipedia.org/wiki/Outliers_(book) (accessed June 6, 2016).

3. Ibid.

4. Tom Corley, 2016. *Change Your Habits, Change Your Life: Strategies That Transformed 177 Average People into Self-Made Millionaires* (Minneapolis: North Loop Books), 52.

5. Shana Lebowitz, 2015. "Science Says People Decide these 13 Things Within Seconds of Meeting You." *Business Insider.* http://www.businessinsider.com/science-of-first-impressions-2015-11/#if-youre-trustworthy-1 (accessed June 11, 2016).

6. Jenna Goudreau, 2016. "A Harvard Psychologist Says People Judge You Based on 2 Criteria When They First Meet You." *Business Insider.* http://www.businessinsider.com/harvard-psychologist-amy-cuddy-how-people-judge-you-2016-1 (accessed June 18, 2016).

7. Janine Willis and Alexander Todorov, 2005. "First Impression: Making Up Your Mind After a 100-Ms Exposure to a Face." Princeton University. http://psych.princeton.edu/psychology/research/todorov/pdf/Willis%26Todorov-PsychScience.pdf (accessed June 6, 2015).

8. Pon Staff, 2011. "Body Language in Negotiation: How Facial Expressions Impact Bargaining Scenarios." *Harvard Law School Daily Blog.* http://www.pon.harvard.edu/daily/negotiation-skills-daily/how-facial-expressions-affect-trust/ (accessed June 6, 2015).

9. "Would I Lie to You? (Engineering Trust with your Face)." *Social Capital Blog.* 2008. https://socialcapital.wordpress.com/2008/08/20/would-i-lie-to-you-engineering-trust-with-your-face/ (accessed June 6, 2015).

10. Pamela Vaughan, 2012. "30 Thought-Provoking Lead Nurturing Stats You Can't Ignore." HubSpot. http://blog.hubspot.com/blog/tabid/6307/bid/30901/30-Thought-Provoking-Lead-Nurturing-Stats-You-Can-t-Ignore.aspx (accessed June 6, 2015).

11. "Conversations That Win Executive Insights." Slideshare. Corporate Visions, 2013. http://www.slideshare.net/CorporateVisions/conversations-that-win-executive-insights (accessed June 6, 2015).

## Chapter 14: The Evolution of Sales Methodologies

1. Tom Corley, 2016. *Change Your Habits, Change Your Life: Strategies That Transformed 177 Average People into Self-Made Millionaires* (Minneapolis: North Loop Books), 52.

2. BuzzBuilder Lead Generation Software, 2013. "20 Shocking Sales Stats That Will Change How You Sell." Slideshare. www.slideshare.net/JakeAtwood1/20-shocking-sales-stats (accessed March 8, 2014).

3. Matthew Dixon and Brent Adamson, 2011. *The Challenger Sale: Taking Control of the Customer Conversation* (New York: Penguin Group), 18.

## Chapter 15: Building a Successful Sales Process

1. Michael E. Gerber, 1995. *The E-Myth Revisited: Why Most Small Businesses Don't Work and What to Do About It* (New York: Harper Business), 221.

2. BuzzBuilder Lead Generation Software, 2013. "20 Shocking Sales Stats That Will Change How You Sell." Slideshare. www.slideshare.net/JakeAtwood1/20-shocking-sales-stats (accessed March 8, 2014).

3. Pamela Vaughan, 2012. "30 Thought-Provoking Lead Nurturing Stats You Can't Ignore." HubSpot. http://blog.hubspot.com/blog/tab-id/6307/bid/30901/30-Thought-Provoking-Lead-Nurturing-Stats-You-Can-t-Ignore.aspx (accessed June 6, 2015).

4. Scott Tousley, 2015. "107 Mind-Blowing Sales Statistics That Will Help You Sell Smarter." Hubspot. https://blog.hubspot.com/sales/sales-statistics (accessed July 17, 2016).

## Chapter 16: Just Say "NO" to Bad Customers

1. Frederick F. Reichheld and Thomas Teal, 1996. *The Loyalty Effect: The Hidden Force Behind Growth, Profits, and Lasting Value* (Boston: Harvard Business School Press).

## Chapter 17: Plan for Job Changes—Starting Now!

1. David Brock, 2014. "A Frightening Look at 'The Cost of a Salesperson.'" *Partners in Excellence Blog.* http://partnersinexcellenceblog.com/a-frightening-look-at-the-cost-of-a-sales-person/ (accessed October 18, 2016).

2. Frederick F. Reichheld and Thomas Teal, 1996. *The Loyalty Effect: The Hidden Force Behind Growth, Profits, and Lasting Value* (Boston: Harvard Business School Press).

3. Emma Brudner, 2014. "The Majority of Salespeople Are Looking for a New Job." Hubspot. https://blog.hubspot.com/sales/salespeople-looking-for-new-job-infographic#sm.0001786vfdc7ydtaxjh2cy491orur (accessed July 24, 2016).

4. Fifth Third Bank, 2016. "Nearly Half of Americans Live Paycheck to Paycheck." *Cision PR Newswire.* http://www.prnewswire.com/news-releases/nearly-half-of-americans-live-paycheck-to-pay-check-300256166.html (accessed July 27, 2016).

5. Jana Kasperkevic, 2015. "100,000 and Up Is Not Enough—Even the 'Rich' Live Paycheck to Paycheck." *The Guardian: Business.* https://www.theguardian.com/business/2015/dec/25/wealthy-americans-living-paycheck-to-paycheck-income-paying-bills (accessed July 29, 2016).

6. Jack Holmes, 2016. "More than Half of Americans Reportedly Have Less than $1,000 to Their Name." *Esquire.* http://www.esquire.com/news-politics/news/a41147/half-of-americans-less-than-1000/ (accessed July 29, 2016).

7. Tom Corley, 2016. *Change Your Habits, Change Your Life: Strategies That Transformed 177 Average People into Self-Made Millionaires* (Minneapolis: North Loop Books), 31.

8.) Ibid.

9. Jennifer Grasz, 2016. "Number of Employers Using Social Media to Screen Candidates Has Increased 500 Percent Over The Last Decade." Career Builder. http://www.careerbuilder.com/share/aboutus/pressreleasesdetail.aspx?sd=4%2f28%2f2016&siteid=cbpr&sc_cmp1=cb_pr945_&id=pr945&ed=12%2f31%2f2016 (accessed July 29, 2016).

## Chapter 18: Raise Millionaire Children

1. Tom Corley, 2016. *Change Your Habits, Change Your Life: Strategies That Transformed 177 Average People into Self-Made Millionaires* (Minneapolis: North Loop Books), 31.

2. Ibid.

3. "A Look at the Shocking Student Loan Debt Statistics for 2017." 2017. Student Loan Hero. https://studentloanhero.com/student-loan-debt-statistics/ (accessed August 9, 2017).

4. Richard Vedder, 2017. "How to Beat the High Cost of Learning." *The Wall Street Journal.* https://www.wsj.com/articles/how-to-beat-the-high-cost-of-learning-1487204060 (accessed March 12, 2017).

5. Biography.com Editors, 2017. "Warren Buffett." A&E Television Networks. https://www.biography.com/people/warren-buffett-9230729 (accessed August 20, 2017).

# ABOUT THE AUTHOR

• • •

Dustin Ruge is an award-winning sales and marketing guru with over twenty years of successful sales, marketing, and management experience. Dustin's experience in sales, marketing, and business strategy ranges from technology start-ups to Fortune 500 companies where he received numerous awards and recognition for his work.

His recent books include *The Successful Sales Manager* and *The Top 20%: Why 80% of Small Businesses Fail at Sales and Marketing and How You Can Succeed.* In addition, Dustin is the author of many articles and professional resources.

Known as one of the most respected and trusted digital sales and marketing strategist/coaches in the nation, Dustin is frequently referenced in major news and trade publications and regularly provides seminars, panel discussions, and keynotes for professional business organizations and associations across the nation. Dustin also hosts The Social Television Network's "Business Leaders" program.

How to follow Dustin:

WEBSITE: DustinRuge.com

FACEBOOK: www.facebook.com/dustinruge/

LINKEDIN: www.linkedin.com/in/dustinruge/

TWITTER: twitter.com/dustinruge

YOUTUBE: YouTube.com: search for "Dustin Ruge"